Fields of Success

Raised Expectations

Dr. Joseph Profit

With

Matthew T. Nebel

Foreword by Joe R. Reeder

Credits:
Cover/Jacket Design by: Mario D'Andre Robinson
Book Formatted by: Wanda McVan
Editors: Sharon Freeman and Becky Holland
Proofreader: Linda McVan

The author may be contacted at the following address:
Dr. Joseph Profit
1266 West Paces Ferry Rd, Suite 317, Atlanta, GA 30327
Phone: 404-236-9230 Fax: 800-893-4307
Email: jp30003@gmail.com

To order this book, contact your local bookstore. You may also place your order at amazon.com, joeprofit.com or call 866-663-2608 Ext. 102.

ISBN-13: 978-1480293090
ISBN-10: 1480293091

I WOULD LIKE TO FIRST DECICATE THIS BOOK
TO THE ONE I LOVE; MY EARTHYLY FATHER,
THE LATE SIMON PROFIT, SR
AND TO MILITARY DAD'S EVERYWHERE!

SIMON PROFIT, SR
United States Army
1938 to 1946
World War II Veteran

DEDICATION

This book is dedicated to my beloved late parents,
Simon and Ethel Profit,
my darling sisters
the late Dr. Pearlie Profit Nabors,
the late Barbara Profit Anderson
and to all of my coaches
the late Patrick H. Robinson, Mackey Freeze, Abe Peirce III,
Harvey B. Simmons, Henry Reeves, the late Eugene Hughes,
the late Dixie B. White and the late Bob Grosclose
to whom I am grateful for many things, especially for pushing me to stay the course and caring enough to teach me the benefits of short term behavior change, the value of diversity and a very good education!

Fields of Success

Raised Expectations

Dr. Joseph Profit

With

Matthew T. Nebel

Foreword by Joe R. Reeder

TABLE OF CONTENTS

	Foreword by Joe R. Reeder	ix
	Introduction: Landing Hard on the Field	xii
1	Growing Up a Profit	Pg 01
2	Lessons in Determination	Pg 15
3	Treading the Thin Line	Pg 33
4	The Power of Expectations	Pg 59
5	Stepping Over the Line	Pg 69
6	The World Against Me	Pg 91
7	Changing Their Minds	Pg 117
	Gallery of Pictures and Articles	Pg 125
8	Determination and Resiliency	Pg 157
9	Two Fields at Once	Pg 181
10	Making a Historical Impact	Pg 201
11	Roadblocks to Stepping Stones	Pg 223
12	Life Keeps Changing	Pg 235
13	Searching for True Success	Pg 241
14	Profit's Views on Life in the Business World	Pg 253
15	Profit's Views on Economics	Pg 263

Acknowledgements

On life's journey no one walks alone. Although there are countless number of people who have motivated, inspired and encouraged me to write this book, just where do I start to thank those that joined me, walked beside me, and helped me along the way continuously urging me to write a book.

First and foremost, I would like to thank my beautiful wife Wanda for standing beside me and encouraging me to share my experiences by writing this book so that it may inspire others on their road to success. She provides me with endless inspiration and she is the one person I can always count on to have limitless patience when my head is in the clouds. Her total commitment to our Heavenly Father, her courageous spirit and her incredible love for me has inspired and strengthened me. She is fearless yet tender, full of joy and passionate. Her love for family is a testament to her parents, the late Clarence and Lena Pearl McVan. Without her steadfast commitment to me I do not believe I could have answered the call to write this book.

Many times after giving a speech, someone from the audience would walk up to me and tell me how much my speech had inspired them and that I should write a book about my life story. So at last, here it is. Perhaps this book will be seen as "thanks" to the tens of thousands of you who have helped make my life what is today.

Much of what I have experienced over the years came as the result of being a product of a segregated society including but not limited to: education, sports and business. Therefore, I would like to thank Northeast Louisiana University (University of Louisiana Monroe) especially the athletic program and the Student Government Association.

I also would like to thank a wonderful man who changed me completely, and that was Coach Bob Groseclose - he taught me humility and how to value the lives, thoughts and expressions of others, how to care for, understand and respect the views of others and their desire to protect their way of life. Sadly he passed on so my thanks go to his wife Jeanne and the entire Groseclose family.

I will also like to express thanks to Matthew T. Nebel, for his dedication to this project, and to Don Zimmerman for his keen eye on the detail events starting in the early years of our development as student's athletes.

Special thanks to all of my children and their spouses and especially my grandchildren, for living lives of commitment and integrity and for supporting my many activities and many travels away from home.

Thanks to all my friends, especially James "Shack" Harris, Goldie Setters, Joe R. Reeder, Louis R. Butler, W.C. Starling, Jr, Pettis Norman, Valerie Martin, Robert Payne, Rubin Jones, Perry Thomas, Ron Hollis, Mr. Robert "Mule" Carter, Theodore and Nora Brown, Richard Brown, Don Warren, Charmaine Polk, Matthew H. Patton, Garland D. Shells, Susan and Tommie Neck, Jim Blackwell, Jimmy and Rosemary Patterson, Mayor Lorenzo "Lo" Walker, Bob Anderson, Keith Prince, Lee and Glenn Weissman, Steve Black, Robert Lee Matthews, the late Ernie "Big Cat" Ladd, and the late Jack Kemp for sharing my happiness and challenges when it seemed too difficult to stay the course. I probably would have not become the person I am today without their support and encouragement.

Thanks to Sharon Freeman, Becky Holland and Linda McVan for their excellent editing and to Mario D'Andre Robinson for the creative cover design.

FOREWORD

By Joe R. Reeder

As an avid, life-long college and professional football fan, I knew Joe Profit's name long before he ever knew mine. I had heard his name in the news and seen him on TV. I had learned his story of adversity, and had seen how he grew into the man he is today. It wasn't until after his days in the NFL that I finally got the privilege to meet Joe, who by then was a prominent Atlanta businessman. But I quickly learned that the person I had seen on TV was only a thin layer of the real Joe Profit.

Following his days as a professional football running back and his short detour through Hollywood, for me, getting to know the "Coach" as a friend, as a father, as my client, and as the inspirational leader he has become has truly been a remarkable experience. I am both honored and delighted to introduce the readers to Joe's autobiography. You, dear reader are in for a great experience.

Joe's indomitable personality and his force of will have allowed him to prevail over countless formidable adversaries and obstacles. Joe redefines the word "perseverance." When I first met him, Joe had taken on one of the world's corporate icons, Southwest Bell, by going after a contract with the United States Army at Sunny Point, North Carolina, one of the world's premier military ammunitions depots. The contracting officers, comforted by working for decades with a corporate icon, did everything in their powers to bypass this determined minority contractor, who was persistent in seeking to "break-in" with the big boys. Joe ultimately prevailed; not only did he win the contract; he won the profound respect of Army officials as well. Sometime later, I again saw this same persistence and ultimate success in La Jolla, California with one of the nation's largest VA research hospitals, and yet again with the General Services Administration (GSA) in Dallas, Texas, the agency that oversaw the wiring and overall communications throughout the Federal courthouse in Stillwater, Oklahoma. In each of these instances, Joe's competence, teamwork, perseverance, infectious goodwill and refusal to ever give up overcame obstacles that, to most others, would have been insurmountable.

Every young person reading this book will enjoy Joe's "mind over matter" philosophy. No matter what the mission, Joe never entertained any excuse for coming up short of success. I saw him hold his own with former President Reagan, whom Joe supported for president, and also with top government presidential appointees. Just a few years back, Joe and I, along with a two others, traveled to New Orleans four days after Hurricane Katrina hit. We stayed there for two hard days—one with an 82nd Air Borne Division squad patrolling New Orleans Sixth Ward, helping human (and animal) victims in the boiling sun and stench in the aftermath of that devastating disaster. For an entire stinking, scorching day, I witnessed Joe first hand, inspire the entire squad of 82nd Airborne soldiers, and uplift the devastated Katrina victims, all of whom Joe called, "My People."

Reminiscing over my years with Joe also reminds me of sobering days I spent with him in a weight room, where Joe consistently showed indefatigable patience and perseverance with those of us who were lesser endowed (and there were many of us). At that time, Joe was runner up in the Mr. Universe 40-and-over bodybuilding competition).

Joe's broad circle of family and friends, his sheer physicality, his spiritual and mental strength, his confidence, his extraordinary sense of humor and his stubborn refusal to quit have always carried him far. This force of nature, as I refer to him, has also carried those of us who have been privileged enough to be around him in battle, or to be on his team. Joe Profit's sheer goodness is infectious, and I think that will be true even for those of you fortunate enough to read this book.

Very few who read this life story, and experience Joe's formula for success, can lay claim to the strength of character that has helped Joe surmount the burdens he has faced and overcome literally from birth. Many readers will never get to know Joe personally, but in reading this book he will lift up every reader by some of the experiences that have come with his remarkable and blessed life.

Enjoy!

Joe R. Reeder
Managing Shareholder, Greenberg Traurig, LLP
United States Under Secretary of the Army (1993-1997)

INTRODUCTION

Landing Hard on the Field

With a quiet thump that nobody else in the stadium seemed to hear, the ball sunk deep into my arms. I had been waiting for it my entire life. I had been waiting for things to get better. In that instant, I simultaneously did three things. I kicked up my right leg and started running forward. I shifted the ball into a snug pocket between my chest and my forearm. Lastly, I began to think. A long road had gotten me to where I was in that instant. It had been a road full of so many lessons and so much continual progress—so many triumphs and failures. The thought of it all was captivating, but I had no more than a flashing moment to let it grace my mind. As I accelerated further down the field, it seemed to wash away in the wake of my footsteps.

I cut left. Going back toward the center of the field, I saw that my blockers had spread open a hole just big enough for me to slide through. With a kick of my left leg, I leaped over one of my blockers' legs. A defender reached out and grabbed my shoulder pads, but I shrugged him off and burst past the wall of linemen.

Now my sights were on the field ahead. There were only a few more defenders to beat, and I knew I had more will to win than they had to take me down. I started lifting my legs faster, and I came into a full sprint. The world brushed past me like the wind, and everything around me whirled into a painted blur. The only things that stayed in place were the stretch of green in front of me, and the pay dirt of the end zone.

It was then that I felt a blow like thunder on my back. My feet became cinder blocks, and I struggled aimlessly to drag myself forward. I knew a defender had broken free from his blocker, and latched onto me. He was pulling me down to the same green grass that had looked so promising only a moment earlier. My knee collided with the earth first. As the rest of my body tumbled to the ground, I still had the ball snug in my hand, and I was soon buried under a pile. The play was over, but the pain was yet to come. Before I could get up off the ground, my tackler grabbed my left leg and extended it backward. It was the worst kind of cheap shot a defensive player could take. A jolt of pain shot through the nerves in my knee, and I cried in pain.

It all took an instant—only a speck of a moment in time—but to me it was my biggest turning point. I looked across the field of my life, and the grass before me started to wither away. It was at that moment when I knew everything I had learned, everything I had done and everything I stood for in every field of my life would be tested. In the instant that I was knocked to the ground, I began again to think of the future. I wondered if I would ever get up. I wondered if I would ever play another game. I wondered what lay ahead for me in that yet unknown field.

It was in the fourth game of my career that I tore my ACL. Only a few months earlier, the Atlanta Falcons had selected me seventh overall in the 1971 NFL draft. As soon as the Falcons selection was made public, a lot of the fans and media in Atlanta began to ask the same question, "Joe *who*?" Not a lot of people had heard of the running back from Northeast Louisiana University, and even fewer people suggested that I would be drafted as early as I was. The widespread skepticism fell like rain pouring down from me from all sides, and all I had done to earn it was play the best football that I could. It didn't seem fair that my rookie season had to be cut so short, but any amount of complaining wouldn't change a thing.

The statistics indicate that over three quarters of professional athletes become financially stressed or bankrupt just two years after retirement. When I got injured, and I lay on the turf clutching my knee, I was presented with two options: push forward and overcome adversity one more time and remain significant, or become a part of that grueling statistic. For many, it wouldn't be such a simple decision. For me, it wasn't a decision at all. I had faced adversity in many forms, all throughout my life, and I had come out a better person every time. By that time in my life, the only thing I knew how to do was push forward.

I believe anyone can achieve success in their own life if they learn to persevere through adversity. I can understand if you don't believe me yet, but all you have to do flip through the following pages and you'll see that it is true. I'll show you the way I've progressed through the three most challenging fields of my life—the cotton field, the football field and the business field—and the way I've grown, learned lessons and achieved success in each one.

In this book, you'll experience the things that molded my life leading up to and through my career-ending NFL injury on the gridiron. I'll take you from my beginnings in the cotton fields of Louisiana, to my overmatched struggles against the racially segregated world of the Jim Crow South, all the way up to my feats of success in business, in the community, and in life. You will see the way Louisiana's color barrier was broken, paving the way for countless African-American athletes who are now playing on the biggest stages in the world. You will learn through my stories that you truly can prevail if you stay strong and focused through adversity. You will learn that success is an endless battle that involves long-term goals with little successes along the way. You'll also learn why I consider that moment lying injured on the football field to be not only the biggest turning point of my life, but also one of the best things that ever happened to me.

One

GROWING UP A PROFIT

Growing Up a Profit with Honor

"Dinner is served!" I heard my mom yell into the hallway. The words shook the house as they blasted through the cracks of our rickety old walls. The trembling power of her voice when she announced dinnertime each night was only ever rivaled by the stampede that would ensue soon after. As soon as the call was heard throughout the house, ten pairs of feet—twenty in all—would storm out their doors and into the hallway, ready to trample anything that stood in their path. The fact that there were so many of us in the family meant that there was no lack of competition. We grew up big and strong not because of how we ate, but rather because we were forced to earn what we ate.

"You've gotta be quick!" My mom would say, Cause there's eleven of us, but there's only enough food for ten!"

That was her little joke. It was her way of dealing with the poverty that had taken over our entire community. She always said you need to make light of the situations—even the worst ones—because if you don't, they're never going to get any better. I always admired that, and I learned from it, but at that time it was hard to envision things getting any better than they were.

The Profit family consisted of my mom, Ethel, my dad, Simon, my four brothers James, Simon Jr., Leroy and David, my four sisters

Purdis, Pearl, Barbara and Annie, and me. I was the fifth child overall, born on August 13, 1949. On that day in history, President Harry Truman and his wife appeared on the cover of LOOK Magazine under the headline "The Negro Problem". The Ku Klux Klan had infiltrated the government in the south, and many minorities from the South had migrated north in hopes of a better life. The problem was that the rapid migration led to widespread unemployment, famine and malnutrition in the north. Very few of the migrants were successful. In response, President Truman and his wife did their best to provide for the minorities of the country, but it was too much of a problem to overcome.

In the long run, it turned out that there wasn't a place in the whole country where a black person was better off, so my family and I kept ourselves in the "Great South" where the lawless Klansmen ran the world. It was in the "Great South" that we had our people and our heritage to lean on—we could turn to each other for support. We all loved each other, because family was all we had. In that time, the only way to survive was to rely on the person seated beside you. You needed their help, because there was no way to change the lawless.

We grew up on a sharecropping farm in Lake Providence, Louisiana, in a home that was built by my dad. It was here that the cotton industry reigned supreme. The few white farm owners made a living, and the countless black and brown workers were left with little more to their names than their ramshackle homes.

You could argue very easily that Lake Providence was a misleading name for the town. Everywhere you looked, there was poverty, pain and hunger and there seemed to be little hope for divine providence. It was, and still is, one of the poorest parishes in the country, with well over half of its families living below the poverty line. Many of those families were either like us, with many children to feed, or they were headed by single parents trying to raise families all on their own. Sometimes they were both. The best you could ever hope for in those days was a good sowing season in the field, so you could earn your share and survive for one more day. After that, all you needed was a little grace from God.

We lived there for the first six years of my life before we moved to Monroe, Louisiana, but we still went back there each summer to pick cotton—the whole family. Even through the years, when one sibling would grow up and move out of the house, they would still come back to the cotton field in the summer. It was a place of meeting—a place that brought us all together as one. It was a very poor, desolate place to live, and sometimes the soil was so dry and cracked that it looked as though there was no hope for the future. But up through those cracks in the dirt, a family was able to grow firm and strong, ready to beat all *odds*.

Lessons in the Cotton Field

The first lessons I learned in life all came from the cotton field. The cotton field was where I got my hands dirty for the first time. It was where I learned to be a strong, hard worker. It was where I learned to be a team member. It is where I learned to be persistent.

When I think of my dad's legacy, I always think of him working hard and earning a living out in the cotton field. That is where I picture him because that is where he spent most of his time, whether he liked it or not. He had to stay in the field to support his family. He would come home at the end of the day with cracked and blistered hands; his sore back and grime-filled face that made it look like the cotton had siphoned all the energy from his body. But it was in those cracks and blisters, along with the sweat, grime and pain that graced our home each evening, that I learned what it meant to have a work ethic. I would watch my dad each evening come home each evening after enduring the ruthless beating of fieldwork, and each morning he would get back up and do it again, despite the awareness that it was slowly bringing him to the ground. If it hadn't been for his wife and nine kids, there would have been no reason for him to do this, but he knew right away that the value in his work transcended his own personal gain. He knew that he was working for all of us—to provide a better life for all of us. That is how I see my dad's legacy. He sacrificed himself so that my brothers, sisters and I could go on and make the world exponentially better.

I remember the day that my dad "hired" me to help him in the field. I was just nine years old, but it had gotten to the point where he just couldn't support us all on his own, so he called on the entire family for help—me, my brothers, sisters and even my mom. Among us, there was no hesitation or questioning. We all had seen dad suffer in the field for us, and we knew it was our turn to return the favor. Even though I was only a small boy and I might not have been the best suited for the job at the time, I was excited that I finally had the opportunity to help my dad.

I remember walking out into the field, trailing behind my dad, trying to keep a handle on the tools as they slid around in my small, nine-year-old hands. It was around five thirty in the morning—well before the sun was up and well before anyone else was out there. My eyes were droopy and I yawned with every step I took. But dad looked wide awake.

"We have to be the first ones in the field each morning," he said, "because that's when you can get the most work done. That's when the cotton is still wet. It makes it easier to handle."

He assigned us each to our own row in the field. To pass the time, we would sing songs that went to the beat of our work. First, we would hear a woman start singing somewhere off in the distance, "This little light of mine . . ." and you would shout back, ". . . I'm gonna let it shine!" After a few verses, you would have the whole field singing along. It was a beautiful sight to see and melodious to hear. There was nothing more magical than a field full of people—poor, blue collar people—coming together as one body and singing, "Let it shine, let it shine, let it shiiiiine!" We always sang songs of grace, songs of praise and songs of hope. That was the only way we kept ourselves working. It was for hope of a better tomorrow.

We wouldn't stop working until the sun was down below the western horizon, and for all that work, I only made four dollars a day. Four dollars. The amount of the money was not the most important thing to me at all; rather it was the virtue that I was carrying my weight. I was giving back to my family and most importantly my dad-someone who had given me more than I could ever repay. I considered those four dollars as a down payment toward developing my work ethic. For that reason, I still consider that four dollars was the best money I ever earned.

In an average day, the best workers in the field could pick about 200 pounds of what we called "seed cotton," the real guts of the product. In a really good day, someone would get close to 300 pounds all by himself. But the average adult man picked about 100 pounds per day, and that was all that was ever expected. I remember the day that I first reached that benchmark. I felt so happy, as a nine-year-old being able to work with the big boys. It was the first time I had seen anything but anguish on my dad's face while we were out in that field. He was so proud of what I had done. I remember smiling back, and realizing that, despite the dirt, grime and sweat that veiled our faces, both of us were beaming like the sun. Just seeing that bit of happiness from him made me want to go back and do it again.

I returned to the field the next day, and my older brother Simon was there waiting for me. His face was covered in grime, too, but there was no light to be found beneath it. "What are you so happy about?" He said.

I kept smiling and said, "Didn't you hear what happened yesterday? I picked my first hundred pounds of cotton."

"Yeah? Well you're the biggest fool in town." "What do you mean?"

He waved his hand over the rest of the field, "You just showed them you can pick a hundred pounds of cotton. Now they'll expect you to keep it up. Every. Single. Day. You just made a big mistake."

I didn't like that he saw it that way. To me, it was the greatest honor to be considered a hard worker like my dad. I longed for that to be a part of my own legacy. I just looked my brother in the eye and said, "You're damn right, I'm gonna keep it up! I just picked a hundred pounds, and I'm about to pick a hundred pounds more!" I stormed past him and went on my way.

Out in the cotton field, I learned what it truly meant to have a work ethic, and my dad was the foundation of it all. There was no room for slacking off and no room for complaints. We did our work because it had to be done. If it didn't get done, we would fail as a family. It was as simple as that.

I learned more from him in that field than anywhere else and from anybody else. He taught me to be responsible. He taught me to keep working until the job gets done, and then go back to your elder and ask what more you can do. Most of all, he taught me that you have to work more for less before you can ever start working less for more. I learned you need to put in the long hours early and often, and even though you won't see any gain from it in the short-term, the payoff will surely come further down the road.

I like to think of my dad as the driving force behind the great things I've been able to accomplish in my life. In that respect, his legacy is alive and strong today. I know he would be proud to see not only the way I've handled myself, but the way that I've given back to the world just as he taught me to do in the cotton field.

My dad's legacy is only multiplied when I factor in my brothers and sisters. They've gone and done great things as well, and it was all because of him. I've tried to emulate him as much as possible, because I've learned that when you devote yourself to making the world better for others—without expecting anything in return—your legacy will shine and multiply forever.

The Influence of My Mom

A lot of my values in life are based on the principles my dad taught me, mainly because I was with him so often after I started working in the fields. But if my dad was the bricks that built our home, then my mom was the mortar that held it all together. She was a small woman, about five feet five, but she was strong in spirit, and she had a backhand that could floor a 200-pound running back.

But even though she had a stern side, it was sweetness and kindness that my mother really brought to the home. She gave us a sense of hope, even in the hardest of hard times, even when it seemed like there was only enough food for ten. I think that kind of hope is crucial to establishing the expectations of a household. When times are rough, it's easy to do two things. The first is to give in—to accept that things are bad and refuse to do anything to change that. It's easy to get in that cycle when our expectations are low, but if we have high expectations then we'll see that the cycle is inconsequential. The second thing we do is blame someone else. I didn't do anything to deserve this. This is a detrimental attitude even if there really is someone else to blame. It does nothing to solve the problem, and does everything to perpetuate the idea that you can't do anything to change it all.

My mother made sure that we never fell into these traps, and she lived it by example as well. She would tell us every morning to get up and work hard, no matter what we had to do. She said if we got up and faced our obstacles, things would be better at the end of the day. And we took her at her word. We didn't question it, because as a black female living in the Deep South at that time, we figured she knew a thing or two about oppression. For her sake, we kept fighting, and while it was hard on everyone, things eventually did get better.

Mom made sure that we never fell into these traps, and she lived it as well. She would tell us every morning to get up and get busy, she would say, "Today is going to be a good day!" She said if we got up and faced our obstacles, things would be better at the end of the day. I remember one early Saturday morning, my mother woke me up that same way, but I refused to get out of bed. I said, "No, today is not going to be a good day. I work six days a week. If I go out into the field again I'll probably keel over and die."

To my complete surprise, my mother said, "Okay, whatever you want, dear," and left me home while she and the rest of the family went to work. At the end of the day, they all returned home and my mother prepared dinner as she did every day after work. It wasn't long before the smell of the food wafted through the hallway and into my nose. I went out to join my family at the dinner table, but when I took my seat, I saw there were only ten dishes at the table. When I reached for another, my mom batted my hand with the serving spoon and said, "Boy, put your butt in that seat. You're going to sit there and watch us, and you're going to learn a lesson: You don't work, you don't eat."

I went to bed without dinner that night, and the next morning when I woke up, my stomach was grumbling. I thought I was going to be sick. But when my mom came in and asked me if I was ready to face the day, I didn't waver. I said, "Yes, Mama," and got my butt out of bed. From that day forward, I never thought to question her word. She had seen a lot of bad days in her life. If she could say it was going to be a good day, I figured I could too.

My Monroe: Two sides of the tracks

In 1955, my dad got a job as a construction worker in Monroe, Louisiana, 75 miles west of Lake Providence. There are approximately 115 Townships, Counties, Cities, towns and Villages that call Monroe home. The city itself was home to about 35,000 people at the time, making it one of the largest city in the state (historically French: Poste-du-Ouachita[1]) the parish seat of Ouachita Parish, Louisiana, United States. But even with the larger population, it still felt like a very small, tightly-knit neighborhood because you could only associate with your own part of the town. What I mean by that is that you had to stay with your color. People like to use the metaphor of "the other side of the tracks". Well, that is literally how it was in Monroe. The black population was concentrated and isolated on the south side of town, and the train tracks that ran past the neighborhood turned the metaphorical racial lines into a reality. Crossing over that line was like venturing into uncharted territory—only scarier, because you knew what danger lay ahead. The blacks and whites did not get along at all, and the danger of crossing over was mutual. I guess that's about the only thing we had in common.

There were only two exceptions of black people who would safely cross over the line. One of them, my then future teacher, Mr. Patrick H. Robinson, would later inspire me to be a pioneer of integration. He was not only brave enough to talk to white men, but he was respected by them as well. He was a man before his time—but I'll get to that a bit later. The only other people who crossed over were male construction workers and female maids for white families. Sometimes that was the only place to find work, so some, including my dad, were forced to take the risk. All the other people were advised to "Stay over here in the black neighborhood. If you stay here, you'll be alright."

Of course, it was hard to be alright under our conditions. Much like Lake Providence, most of the families which did have work were still single mothers or single fathers who were trying to raise their children all on their own. Those families earned an average of $800-$1000 each month-not nearly enough to support a healthy family. The streets were laden with broken-down houses and broken-down families. It was in times like these that my mother's words gave me the comfort I needed. She often said, "You make light of the situation, and things will get better."

Through the financial struggles, people seemed to find strength in the structure of their community. Monroe was good in that sense—powerful, even. The black neighborhood was small, but individuals supported each other personally and socially; it was this interdependence that allowed us to survive. There were many advantages the white community had over us, but I truly think this sense of community is one advantage we had over them.

Growing up in Monroe

Though it wasn't much to look at to an outsider, Monroe was a breeding ground for successful athletes. Actually, I take that back. The city as a whole had brought about its fair share of successful athletes, but the real breeding ground was more specific. It was isolated into a small, eight-block neighborhood called Bryant's Addition, a truly special place in America. Over the course of history, more than one hundred athletes from Bryant's Addition have signed contracts with the NFL, the NBA or the Harlem Globetrotters. People from the outside claim that there must be something in the water—something that gives the people a magical ability—but in reality there is nothing more than high expectations and the guiding hand of God.

Bryant's addition, as luck would have it, is where my family lived. I attended a school named Swayze Jr. High School. Swayze was one of the five schools in Monroe that served black children at the primary level, but it was unique, because it was the only one that had a football team. Looking back, I realize how blessed I was that I was able to go there. The founder of the athletic program was someone I mentioned earlier- Mr. Patrick H. Robinson.

Mr. Robinson, put simply, was a man well-ahead of his time in Monroe. Although he was black, he was respected and loved by both blacks and whites in a time where blacks were conditioned to submit to whites and stay out of the way whenever possible. Despite these rules, he stood tall, looked every man square in the eye and spoke exactly what was on his mind.

He truly was a hero for our school, and for us children. On the field and off the field, he instilled in us a sense of pride and self-respect. He taught us the value of a good education, and the importance of pursuing knowledge all throughout our lives. He told us to go to college—a concept that was just as foreign to us as crossing over into the white community.

Mr. Robinson became a powerful influence in my life. When I saw the way that he would approach a white businessman, for example, and saw the way he spoke as though they were equals -it blew my mind. I had never before been exposed to that kind of paradigm. I didn't even think it was possible, and neither did most of the people in my neighborhood. But Mr. Robinson loved it! Every once in a while, when we were curious enough, he would teach us a lesson on change. He would say, "You kids are the ones that will help change the culture in this city. You are the ones that will make a difference." I loved that idea. I pictured myself all grown up, standing tall in a nice suit, side-by-side with the most respected people in town. It ignited a fire in me, one that inspired me to push the boundaries of my society, and even cross them. Later down the line, I would take these lessons and put them into practice.

TWO

LESSONS IN DETERMINATION

Following a Legend

Before I ever set foot in the halls of the school, my brother Simon was the football star at Swayze Jr. High. I remember watching him in his first games. When he got the ball, he would zip by in a blur, and I could almost feel the wind crack off of his body when he hit supersonic speed. For me, there was nothing cooler than that, than being the younger brother of the football star. I looked up to him, and even tried to emulate him in every way possible.

Of course, since I was younger, this was not an easy task. His legs were like stilts compared to my little stumps, and he could run circles around me before I even realized he was there. For all I knew, he was the fastest kid in Louisiana. One day while we were walking home together, I asked him, "Simon?"

"Yeah, Lil Joe?" That's what he called me back then. I didn't like it so much at the time, but the name spread until everyone around town knew me as Lil Joe. That was the power my brother had.

"What's your secret?" I asked. "How'd you get so fast?"

"I don't know . . . by eating my vegetables."

"That's a bunch of bull, and you know it!"

He laughed and said, "Yeah, so? There is no secret. You just gotta run fast. One day, you'll grow longer legs and you'll be fast too."

"You mean as fast as you?"

"Well, nobody's ever going to be as fast as me."

"Why not?"

He stopped at the corner of the street, and then he bent down and said, "Okay, Lil Joe, I'll admit it. The truth is that I do have a secret."

"What is it? What is it?"

He laughed, "Not so loud! It's a secret for a reason. You don't want to give it away, do you?" at that time that I was practically jumping, I was so excited. My brother patted me on the shoulder to calm me down. He bent down to one knee to get to my level, though he was still a head taller than me. "Alright. I'll tell you, but you have to swear not to tell anyone else."

"I swear." "For as long as you live?"

"I swear!" I said.

"Okay," he leaned in and whispered, "It's all in the shoes."

I looked down. On his feet was the only pair of sneakers he owned. Back then, none of the parents of the team could afford football cleats, so the children wore their sneakers instead. James' sneakers were just about the ugliest couple of excuses for shoes I had ever seen. Their seams were mangled and frayed. The mesh on the sides clung for dear life by a couple of haphazard threads. The soles were peeling off, and flopped at random when he kicked up his feet.

"Those things?" I said. "I don't believe you."

"Fine," he stood up, "Don't believe in the shoes if you don't want to, but you'll have a hard time proving me wrong if you can't catch me." He let go of my shoulder and took off running. We were still blocks away from my house, but he was halfway there by the time I started chasing after him. I was already winded when I reached the next corner, so I stopped to catch my breath. With my hand on my knees, panting, I turned around and saw the spot where we both had been standing. It may have been the heat that made a mirage, but I swear I could see a trail of burning rubber where he had left my side. From that moment, I believed.

"The shoes," I said, and I took off running again.

Now it was my first day of practice. It was early in the evening after school, and I was running around my house, rifling through closets and dressers, and not bothering to clean up any of the mess that I left in my way.

Finally my mom saw me running through the hallway. I sped past her in the doorway, and she hooked me by the shirt collar (she was the only one that could ever catch me from behind). She spun me around and held me up to her face. Her eyes were pointed, like harpoons ready to fire. She said, "Boy, what on earth are you doing? You're messing up my house!"

I said, "I got practice and I can't find a pair of sneakers."

"What sneakers?"

"Simon's old sneakers. I need them."

"You mean you want to wear those old piles of dirt Simon used to wear?"

"He told me I could have them when I grew up."

My mom just tugged at my shirt, and brought me over to the hallway closet. She opened up the door and reached for the highest shelf. She was still taller than me, but I was growing a lot by this point, and I could see the tip of those familiar laces hanging off the edge of the shelf.

"The shoes," I said, just like I had on the street corner years earlier. But as my mom pulled them down off the shelf, a cloud of dust came with her. She held them out with one hand, far away from her face—and for good reason, as there was the most foul stench seeping out of those once-glorious sneakers. I plugged my nose, and then carefully reached out my free hand to take hold of the laces, but as I did, the soles broke free and fell straight to the floor. We looked down, and then we looked at each other.

"I guess I'll throw them away," I said. I picked up the rubble and took it over to the garbage.

"If not that, then burn 'em in a fire!" Mom turned away and walked back down the hall toward the kitchen.

As I mentioned, none of the children on my team were able to afford good football gear back in those days, so they had to wear sneakers instead of cleats. My family, on the other hand, was so poor that I couldn't even afford a pair of sneakers. Since Simon's shoes were now slowly decomposing in a junk yard, we were completely out of options. My mom told me, despite this, to straighten up and be proud. I tried to listen, but I'll just say that it was hard to find the pride within me as I showed up to my first day of practice in an old pair of work boots.

My good friend, Don Zimmerman, caught up to me as I was treading out onto the field.

"Lil Joe," He said. By this time, I had grown enough that the name Lil Joe didn't fit, but I guess it stuck with me. "Lil Joe, why don't you have your sneakers?"

Don was always a good guy to me. I knew he wouldn't make fun of me for not being able to afford sneakers. I knew most everyone would understand, being from the same kind of home as me. But it was still difficult to think of everyone noticing. I looked down to avoid it all, but that only meant I was staring straight at the boots themselves.

"I can't get sneakers." I said. "Not enough money."

"Didn't you have a pair already?"

"No."

Don could tell I was saddened, so he dropped the issue at that. He just patted me on the shoulder and said, "Don't worry about it."

But it was hard not to worry about it. I didn't want to be poorer than everyone else on the team. Even more, I didn't want everyone to see that I was poorer. I told him, "Thanks," and we both walked over to the group of players forming around Mr. Robinson.

Of course, my teammates did notice my shoes. To be honest, it was hard not to notice them. They were bulky and heavy, and they weighed me down as I walked. They sent shockwaves through the ground and made it shake like an earthquake.

That was their first impression. They were an eyesore and a distraction to everyone on the team. But it wasn't long before I found out that the shoes were my greatest strength. They were heavy, but that only meant that my legs had to work harder in practice, which made them grow stronger than anyone else on the team. The treads on the bottom were all worn down, which caused me to slip on the grass, but that just taught me to keep a lower center of balance. They challenged me to jump harder and run faster just to compensate. I began to grow faster than all of my teammates. Before long, I ran so fast that I outran my old nickname. Lil Joe had left Monroe, and Joe the Jet had come to take his place.

Best of all, with every step I took; they sent a warning call into the great wide open. My adversaries learned quickly to get out of the way when they heard those cloppers coming in their direction. Otherwise, they could prepare for a world of pain. In the end, I saw that the boots were an asset and not a liability. I became the most intimidating thing in town—far more intimidating than anyone could have ever been in a pair of sneakers or a pair of cleats.

The Only Game

Because there was only one team in the area, it meant there weren't a whole lot of options for competitors. We found ourselves having to look inward, playing nearly all of our 'games' as a scrimmage against our own players.

But one day, Mr. Robinson brought us into a huddle and explained that he had managed to schedule a game—a real game. We were going to be playing against Boley Jr. High of West Monroe. I didn't know a lot about West Monroe aside from the fact that it was on the other side of the bridge—and not a lot of people from our neighborhood went over there. But Mr. Robinson knew the area. He crossed the bridge frequently, just like he crossed the train tracks. He told us that Boley was just another black school that didn't have a lot of money, like us. They were a humble team, and all they wanted was a little competition.

Well, we soon found out that they didn't only have slim pickings for competition—they were also short on players for their own roster. We were told this the day before the game. It came as bad news, since we figured they would not be able to play, and we had been relishing the idea of putting our skills to the test of outside competition. But then Coach told us something else—something that made our hearts stop. They were still going to play us, it seemed, but they were going to fill their roster with freshmen and sophomores from West Monroe High School.

The players were so big they looked like giants. As my family and I approached the field on the day of the game, I could almost see them over the tree line. If my legs hadn't been latched down by the awesome weight of my work boots (which added a good five pounds to my body) I would have been shaking at the knees.

I got to the field and went up to Don, who was lacing up his old pair of sneakers. I saw that he was preoccupied examining the other team, too. Don was on the depth chart at quarterback for the day, but he looked like he'd rather be back at home.

"Look at these guys," he said.

"I know. They're gonna plow us into the ground. I hope the field's soft today, at least."

"Yeah, then it won't take them long to dig our graves. It'll be nice and painless."

Our parents had all lined up along the sidelines, ready to cheer us on. It was a new experience for them, too, since they had never had a common adversary either. But when I saw my mom and dad—waving to me and grinning—I couldn't figure in my mind why any parent would want to be a witness to their own child's execution.

Mr. Robinson finally called us over to the huddle. He started his pep talk by addressing us in a way he never had before. "Young men," he said, "It's easy to see that those guys are bigger than you. But you've been playing together for a lot longer than they have. You've got better teamwork; you've got more heart, and you've got more determination."

As coach spoke, he pounded his fist against his palm, stressing the qualities that made us a greater team—at least by his definition. "So I want you to go out there and show them what it means to be a real team! Everybody in!" We all put our hands in the middle. "Swayze, on three, alright? One! Two! Three! Swayze!" Coach was louder than anyone else. Some of us cheered, but they were dull cheers, forced from bottoms of our reluctant hearts.

We hit the field with even less enthusiasm. As we lined up in kickoff formation, their shadows stretched across the field, like dark monsters reaching for the ball. Once the ball was in play, they started playing like monsters, too. Their blockers immediately blasted through our wall as though we were no more than a breeze of wind. Their kick returner took the ball well past midfield before two of our guys were able to rope him down. Only a few plays later, they punched the ball in for their first touchdown.

And then it happened again. The next time they got the ball, they scored on their very first play. The drive after that was the same story. By halftime, the score didn't even matter anymore. Everyone on hand to witness the slaughter knew that the game was no contest. The parents didn't seem to be bothered, but that only made us more frustrated. We began punishing ourselves.

But Mr. Robinson didn't like that kind of behavior. Even with the score the way it was, and even with the kind of game we were playing at the time, he still demanded that we kept at it. He told us he wanted to see some progress.

We got the ball to start the second half. I remember Don pulling us into the huddle.

"We're going to run the 235 play." He said. The 235 play was a simple play—just a full-power fullback run up the middle. My job was to be the lead blocker for the fullback, once the line was able to create a gap.

We broke from the huddle and spread into our formation with no wide receivers or tight ends lined up wide. It was no secret to anyone that we were going to run, but we were hoping that somehow we would be able to find a hole big enough to pick up a few yards. Our fullback's name was Lou Hill. He was one of the biggest guys on our team, so we called him 'The Bull,' but at that time, he looked less like a bull and more like a newborn calf. In comparison, their defense looked like a pack of beasts, chained to a pole but ready to break free at any moment.

Don called out the cadence. My fingers twitched anxiously. I eyed the spot we were aiming to run through—right between the left guard and tackle. That gap between them looked like a mile away.

Finally, the ball was snapped. I lunged forward with my great big thumper shoes and plunged in between the two blockers with The Bull trailing close behind. I felt my face smack into a wall of concrete, and then I felt my whole body hit the ground. As I shifted to see who was on top of me, I saw that it was The Bull. We had both made it past the line of scrimmage, and he still had the ball. A one yard gain.

When we got back to the huddle, Don said, "Alright, let's run 235 again." We snapped the ball and gained another four yards. Then Don took us back to the huddle, said, "235!" and clapped his hands. This time we ran for six more yards and a first down. Over and over again, we ran the 235 play, and each time, we got a face full of concrete. But we marched our way down the field and on the last play of the drive, The Bull and I dove into the end zone for our first touchdown.

We never came close to matching their play at any point in the game. However, by then, it didn't matter to us. By the final quarter, we felt it an accomplishment that we were still on our feet.

Late in the fourth quarter, they had the ball deep into our territory for what seemed like the hundredth time of the game. Whatever demon they had yet to slay, I don't know, but they were still intent on slaying it with a vengeance.

They lined up with no receivers, just like we had with the 235 play. And just like the 235 play, we knew what was going to happen. They were going to run the Green Bay Packers power sweep and run over our defense one more time. On top of that, we knew who was going to get the ball. It was their big, chunky sophomore. So far he had trampled us like an elephant over fleas. It was his size, and not his speed, that made it impossible to bring him down.

I took my place at the linebacker position and bent low to the ground. My work boots were planted firmly in the paint of the 10-yard line and my fingers started twitching again. Earlier in the game he had made mincemeat out of me—on several occasions. I would see him coming and try for a tackle, but I would simply graze off him when I did.

This time, he was just as quick off the snap. He blasted through the line with ease and once again came at me. At that moment, the sophomore turned into a freight train, and the hash marks on the field were the tracks leading straight to my body. He looked fearsome, but still I did not back down. With such little time in the game, I figured I should try to stand my ground. As he approached, I lunged forward again. I saw his dark, mean eyes staring right back at me, and I was sure I was looking hell in the face.

I woke up with my back to the ground. I looked to my side and saw I was in the end zone. Then I heard Don's voice and saw his face appear above me.

"Joe, that was amazing!" He said.

I looked around. Others were walking up to me and asking if I was okay. I brushed them aside and looked back to Don, "What happened? Did I stop him?" "Hell no!" He shouted, "He scored big time! But Joe, you brought him to the ground!" He offered me a hand, and pulled me up to my feet. "Come on, the game's over. Let's head home."

I still don't remember what the score of the game was that day. I'm sure anyone keeping score would have run out of room on their scorecard pretty quickly. All I do remember is that I expected to see a giant crater where I had been plastered to the ground, but there was none. As I limped home next to Don, I said, "Looks like the ground wasn't all that soft."

We got thumped pretty badly that day, but I learned a few things. I learned that you can always find competition that's better than you are. I learned that it's important to stand up to your competition, no matter how big of a shadow they cast. I also learned that you can take your losses in stride. Though we never played another game aside from our own team, the game against Boley reminded us that there would be bigger, tougher teams once we got to high school. We took that lesson and brought it with us. We used it as motivation.

The Free Market

Swayze Jr. High is where I got my start in the world of organized football, but off the field, Swayze Jr. High is where I got my start in the world of organized crime. I called it entrepreneurship. I realized from the outset that I had a gift for recognizing opportunity. When I saw a need in the community, I immediately pounced on the opportunity to help in any way I could. It's just that sometimes I felt it was necessary to add a small price markup on the side.

Take the youngsters in my town, for example. My neighborhood in Monroe was as close as a family. Everyone knew everyone. The proverb, "It takes a village to raise a child" described our community. Sometimes, that wasn't the greatest thing. If a neighbor ever saw you misbehaving while you were out in the street, they would have no problem coming over and whipping your butt straight, and once you got home, you'd get whipped again. So while we children "learned our lessons," we also learned that by looking out for one another, we could avoid getting into trouble.

Naturally, I recognized the potential of this untapped industry. I realized I could make some money if I made it into a business. I made it my duty to learn everything I could while out on the playground. What were people up to? Who had gotten in trouble? Were there any secrets that nobody was supposed to know about? In no time at all, the playground was my own. Any body's secret was my secret too. Any body's folly was my own fortune. I started collecting insurance money from all the children who got into trouble each day. If you didn't want your parents to find out you'd done something wrong, then you had better pay your dues. At free time, I would watch over my kingdom and bask in the beauty of the truly unmediated free market that I had dominated. Some called it blackmail. Some called it bribery. I, on the other hand, referred to it as my very first business.

That's how I was back in that day. I may have had some questionable ethics for a junior high school student, but I always had the heart of a businessman deep inside me. Throughout the rest of my school days, it would show up in random ways, at what seemed like the most ludicrous of times (I'll get to the pigeons and crawfish stories later)—but it all started here, as a young entrepreneur at Swayze Jr. High.

Eventually, I was found out, and I learned the hard way that all dynasties must come to an end. The day after I got out of my business, I was called by Mr. Robinson to go meet with him after school. That's when he explained to me everything that he did outside the walls of Swayze.

"I'm a certified public accountant." He said. "Do you have any idea what that means?" I shook my head, no. He made it sound like something scary the way he said it. The fact that I was called in to meet with a grown up (never a good sign) made me think I was in line for a whooping. But Mr. Robinson smiled and went on, "It means I work with numbers. I do a lot of math for people who don't want to do it themselves."

"What kind of math?" I said.

"Well, math with money. I help people sort out their money, and make sure everything's in order. Basically, I make it easier for people to manage their money."

At the time, the concept didn't really make a lot of sense to me. I had never even seen enough money where I would have said, "That needs to be managed and organized," let alone, if I had seen that much money, I never would have paid someone more money to organize it. All I could say was, "That seems weird."

Mr. Robinson laughed, "Well, I guess it does seem a little weird, but people seem to need the service, so I provide it for them. It's called supply and demand."

"I've heard of that," I said.

"Right. Basically, it means when you have a supply of something that a lot of other people demand, you can start charging them money for it. Supply and demand, see?" He held up both of his hands like a scale, as if he were weighing the two against each other. "It's the foundational principle for the entire economy, more or less. And it works a lot like your little . . . business endeavor from the other day. I've noticed you've got a little businessman in you."

That's when I realized why he brought me in there. I was in deep trouble. What's more, there was no way in hell I was going to get anyone to cover up for me. I sprang forward in my chair and started to explain, "Mr. Robinson, you don't know the whole story. I—"

But he held up one of the hands and pressed it forward, telling me to stop. "It's okay, Joe," he laughed, "I just wanted to talk to you about your future."

It was a little confusing to me. Now he was making it seem like a good thing. "I didn't know taking money from kids would be able to pay off," I said.

"Well, don't make a habit of it. That kind of treatment will get you into trouble in the real world. I want to teach you how to use supply and demand to your advantage—to your healthy and legal advantage. 'Cause Joe, I've seen the fire in your eyes. I've seen the drive you have to excel at anything and everything you do. It's a great quality, and very few people seem to possess it."

"So what do I do with it?" I ask.

"See what you did that got you in trouble?"

"Yeah?"

"Do the opposite of that."

As soon as he said that, my muscles eased up, and I was able to relax. I eased back into my seat, and released my hands from their vice grips on the arms of the chair.

Mr. Robinson continued to explain the basic principles of economics. He taught me that if I used my skills in the right way, I could actually help people instead of using them for my own personal gain. I liked that. It seemed like throughout my whole life, the whole world was comprised of people who were out to get me. I guess it was a relief to know that there were people like Mr. Robinson in the world, who truly had a passion for making things better.

Mr. Robinson was my hero from that day forward. He showed me what it meant to be successful—in a career and in life. He was the only black CPA in town, and he was one of the only successful black people in town. He was the example that I needed. He was the example that showed me anything was possible.

The Pigeon Shuffle: Early Beginnings as a Entrepreneur

After that meeting, my heart started burning for business. It was the very first time in my life that I had been opened to the potential of my talents. In the spring of my eighth grade year, I learned to domesticate those talents, and apply them to more healthy ventures.

And I mean "domesticate" literally. My next venture came to be known as The Pigeon Shuffle. Throughout my life, I had worked with pigeons at the sharecropping house in Lake Providence. We had a whole coop of them, and we would train them to do just about anything—racing, carrying, or just for show. Back then, there was nothing you could boast more than a good show pigeon.

But once we moved down to Monroe, out of the field and into the city, the familiar presence of pigeons became a thing of the past. When I first told my friends that I had trained pigeons on a farm, they scoffed at the idea; they called it gross, and said only country folk did that sort of thing. However, I knew that I could change their minds if I could only get them out in the field.

I riled up a group of young men I knew from the neighborhood. Not all of them were my friends—most of them were actually older than me-but they knew my older brothers, and they knew what type of people came with the name Profit. As a matter of fact, you could have asked anyone in town, they would have said the same thing, "Profits are leaders."

One evening, I laced up my work boots and told them to gather a couple of fishing nets and some bird cages, and meet me at the railroad tracks. I had been along those tracks many times before. I was fond of them because they brought me out of the town and back into the wilderness where I felt comfortable. During some of my long walks, I would notice that there was a lot of garbage left along the sides of the tracks. People would go out there and litter because they couldn't really get caught. Although it pained me to see all the pollution, there were other things on my mind. I knew that pigeons were attracted to garbage. When I saw the garbage, I only thought to myself, "The supply is out there somewhere."

My crew followed me like a wise teacher. Every now and then, if I thought I heard a call, I would stop to listen, and they would stop too. Then, just like a sergeant with his soldiers, I would start up again and they would trail right along behind me.

The first pigeon we saw was rustling its head inside an old candy wrapper. It was the most determined bird I had ever seen, trying to leave no resources unused. But to me, the hunter, it was a golden opportunity.

Then, one of the guys said, "Joe! There's a pigeon right there!"

I swiveled around and smacked him on the head. "Shhh! You tryin' to scare him away?"

Luckily, the pigeon didn't even flinch. I motioned for one of them to hand me a fishing net, then slowly shuffled myself around to the other side of the tracks. I knew I had to be careful, because the ground was sprawled with gravel, and my boots were so big that a step too large could have thrown a train in Mississippi off its rails.

I came around to the pigeon's back, and it was still indulged completely in the candy wrapper. It hadn't even noticed I was there. As a predator circling my prey, I almost felt insulted. It was too easy. When I was within two feet of the pigeon, I looked to the guys, who were all huddled at the other side of the tracks, and I smiled. "Watch this," I mouthed.

The net in both hands, I swiped it down, flipped it over, and brought it back up. If you had only been watching that one spot on the ground where the pigeon had just been, you would have sworn that it just disappeared. Only the candy wrapper remained, and it fluttered slowly to the ground. Up in the net was my prize of the day. I clamped my right hand around the edge of the netting to seal the deal, then looked at my guys and smiled.

That moment marked an explosion in pigeon-hunting enthusiasm in the town of Monroe. It seemed that there was a hunter in every one of those guys, but the city had sucked it out of them. Once they escaped into the country, it all seemed to come flooding back. I taught the art of pigeon catching to anyone willing to learn, and soon had my own industry. We would take groups of people out to the tracks, catch a load of pigeons, and then take them back into town where we would train them for sale just like I had at the farm.

Once the word got out—and word spread like wildfire to the youngsters of that town—the demand for pigeons skyrocketed into oblivion. Who would have thought that a bunch of city boys could have gotten so much of a thrill out of a job that only appealed to country folk?

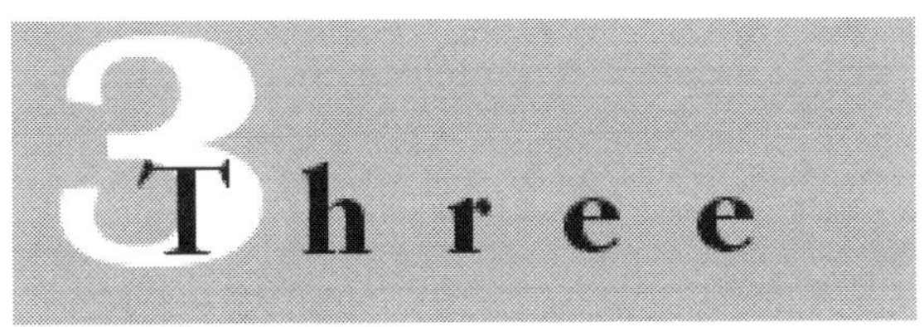

TREADING THE THIN LINE

Uncharted Territory

It was a big summer for me, the summer of 1963. I was preparing to make the leap from junior high to high school, and with that came a lot of raised expectations. My family and I once again returned to Lake Providence to work in the fields for the bulk of our time, and by then, I was a big enough hand that my dad started using me for all the hardest jobs—the manly jobs, as he called them. I felt proud that he was beginning to see me as a man, and I was enthusiastic about being able to help. Every time I was seen working with alongside the big boys, I felt like I was holding a trophy in my hand.

While I kept growing throughout the summer as we worked hard in the fields, the rest of America was growing as well. At the beginning of the summer, President Kennedy made a loud and clear declaration that he would send a civil rights bill through congress making segregation against the law. Meanwhile, the senators and congressmen from the South were in an uproar, as were some of the white workers protesting the movement, and the whole world, as far as I knew it, was divided in two.

In Lake Providence, we were isolated from a lot of the hatred because we were isolated from the rest of society. Pretty much anyone in town was a hand in the field, and once we went out into the field each morning, we were too far away from the rest of the world to care.

But when we returned to Monroe, it was another story. We were thrust back into the early beginnings of the civil rights movement. I quickly learned that matters were escalating all across the south. There were protests from both sides and there were riots in many southern cities. It seemed, for the first time, that the pot was starting to boil.

One day, when my friends and I were walking down a busy city street, we were stopped by a policeman. He pulled his car up to the curb and told us to stay where we were. I started scanning my mind, trying to figure out what I had done wrong, but it didn't seem that there was anything he had against me.

My friends beside me were shaking in fear, but I told them to let me do all of the talking, and to keep calm. That's one thing my dad had always taught me. Keep calm. Don't do anything stupid. If the white man ever threatens you, you treat him with respect. I never knew why he taught me that—it seemed weird to me, to stand down instead of stand up—but I followed my dad's orders. I let the officer speak first.

"What are you boys doing around this neighborhood?"

I didn't know what he meant. It was one of the black neighborhoods. It was close to the line, but I had never had a problem walking down that street.

"Well, officer," I said, "We were just walking around town. And maybe planning on getting a bite to eat somewhere."

"I see," he said. He was wearing a pair of thick sunglasses that made it hard to tell who he was looking at. From any angle, it seemed as though he was looking at all of three of us at the same time. He continued, "And by maybe, you mean you were loitering, weren't you?"

Loitering? I had never heard the word in my life. I responded in a way I felt was intelligent, but I found out later that it wasn't one of the smartest moves I could have made. "I'm sorry, sir," I said, "I don't really know what that means."

He just exhaled through his gritted teeth. The smell hit my face and almost made me gag, but I was able to keep my composure. "Well," he said, "I guess we're going to find out, aren't we?"

I still had no idea what he meant. It was like he was speaking another language. But when he reached around to the back of his belt, he pulled out an object that needed no translation. A pair of handcuffs. When I saw the glint of the sun in the chain, my heart started pounding beneath my shirt. I was thinking, My God, I don't know what I've done, but my daddy's going to whip me good when he hears about this. I quickly started thinking of words to argue, but I caught my tongue before I had a chance to make things even worse.

Without any explanation, he strapped each of our hands behind our backs and shoveled us into the back of his car. I could feel the heartbeats of each of my friends by my side. The car was hot. They were both sweating buckets, and I wasn't far behind them. I just kept reminding them under my breath, "Keep your mouth shut. Don't do anything you're going to regret."

The officer took us down to the courthouse on the white side of town. It was probably the deepest I had ever been in that part of Monroe. Everything we passed on the way there was new to me. The officer pulled the door open and ordered us to get out of the car. The fresh air gave us little relief. It seemed that the sun was hotter on the white side of town, as though it too had turned against us.

Without ever saying a word, we were taken into the courthouse. The officer informed us that we would have to beg our cases in front of a judge. We all looked at each other with faces so pasty you would have sworn we were from the area. Finally, I spoke, "But sir, how can we plead our cases if we don't know what we did wrong?" It seemed like a fair question, but the officer almost flipped his lid.

"I told you boys, you were loitering!"

I decided to leave it at that. The last thing I needed was a tacked on charge of resisting an officer or God knows what else he could invent. My friends and I again reverted to silence. We were brought into the courtroom soon after, and my friends were seated as if to imply that I would be first to go on trial. Standing there all alone, I could only think about how ridiculous it was that I was standing there. I was fourteen years old; I was a well-behaved boy, and here I was standing in a courtroom in handcuffs.

Finally, the judge entered the room. He was even whiter than the officer. He looked as though he had never seen the light of day. He also wore a sharp frown that could have easily cut through my handcuffs.

"All rise!" I heard someone yell from the back of the room. It was at that time that I realized the severity of the situation. It was then that I was truly on trial.

When the judge took his seat, and the rest of the courtroom did the same, I naturally followed along, but then the judge banged his gavel. BAM! I jerked my head.

"You will remain standing, young man!" He shouted. His words echoed endlessly off the walls of the courtroom, making it seem like there were hundreds of judges yelling at me from all different directions. I quickly struggled back to my feet.

He read my case off a sheet of paper in front of him, "We have Mr. Joseph Profit here today on one count of loitering, and one count of unlawful thinking."

The last part made me cringe. Not only had he tacked on an additional charge, but the additional charge made even less sense than the first one. I approached the bench and blurted out, "Unlawful thinking, sir?! What does—?!"

BAM!

It was my worst move of the day by far. After the judge banged his gavel, he leaned forward from his seat and peered down on me. I could see into his nose as his nostrils flared. From up there on the bench he looked about a hundred feet tall, and I felt as small as a bug.

"It is clear to me that we have a pretty bad troublemaker here. I have you here on two accounts—loitering and unlawful thinking. There is overwhelming evidence from our police officer stating that you engaged in lustful behavior toward a group of young females. Therefore, I have no option but to give you thirty days in juvenile detention!"

BAM!

This time, the gavel was a hammer that drove a nail through my heart. I felt like I was in a terrible nightmare, but the cold touch of the handcuffs on my wrists reminded me that it was all real. When I heard the echoes of my final sentence die away in the walls, I started to cry.

Then I felt a hand on my shoulder. It was the public defender. I hadn't seen him speak a word the whole time, though there really wasn't a lot of time to begin with. "Joe," he whispered in my ear, "Don't you worry. I know this judge well, and I know that he's a complete crock. I've seen dozens of people just like you get thrown under the bus by these two guys." He pointed to the judge and the police officer. He said, "You just let me deal with everything. I'll make it all better."

I sniffled back a giant tear. I was so heartbroken, even though I knew I had done nothing wrong. Maybe that was what hurt me the most. I nodded my head, and through my tears I said, "Can I go sit down now?"

"Of course. Don't worry, Joe, that gavel can't touch you anymore."

I felt a strange mix of emotions. It was one of the first times in my life that I had experienced the full-on force of discrimination. I was mad at the white people, because I thought they were to blame. On the other hand, I could hardly comprehend that a white person was coming to my rescue.

I was escorted from the courtroom, and my two friends joined me soon after. They had all received the same sentence as me, and neither of them was taking it very well. Neither was I. I didn't even know what would happen next. Would my parents come see me? Would I go straight to jail? Was it possible to reverse the sentencing? All of these questions raced through my mind, though I still hadn't found out the answer to the most important one: What in the hell were loitering and unlawful thinking?

I sat with my friends for quite some time in a hot, sticky room, but the sweat from the heat didn't compare to the sweat from our anxiety.

Finally, the public defender came through the door. He was smiling. "Good news," he said, "You boys are free to go."

We looked at one another, confused. We were arrested, convicted of a crime we didn't know existed, then released all in a matter of minutes. It was like we were on some crazy game show.

"That's it?" I said.

"Well, it's a bit more complicated than that. I was able to argue with the judge. I told him there was no proof of any unlawful thinking; therefore he couldn't convict you boys. But . . . the only thing is that he's still giving you each a month of probation."

Probation seemed like a day at the spa after what we had just gone through. My friends and I shook hands with the public defender, and gave a million words of thanks. I don't think he knew how much it meant to us.

"I was just trying to help." He said, "I've seen boys like you get thrown away. Good boys. Now, I don't know about this whole segregation thing, but do I know that throwing good boys in jail is wrong. Now why don't you boys get out of here and go on home."

We were released from our handcuffs and made to sign some papers, but after that we were free. The only problem we saw was getting back to the black side of town without something even worse happening on the street. We figured that with our newly-acquired probation, and a second incident in the same day, the judge would not be so kind to us.

Before leaving, the public defender asked if there was anything else we needed. We figured a ride home was too much to ask—he had already done enough—so I simply said, "Could you please just tell us what we were charged for?"

The man explained that we were first charged with loitering, which meant we were standing on public property and refusing to leave. I told him that that was a load of bull, and he agreed. The second charge was unlawful thinking. He explained that many southern cities, including Monroe, had laws against lustful behavior. It was really just there so policemen would have an excuse to arrest a black man. The law stated that if any officer saw you trailing behind a group of ladies, they could technically arrest you for lustful behavior. That's the reason we were charged.

"But we weren't doing any of those things. There weren't even any women around at the time!" I practically shouted.

"And that's what I told the judge. I said if he couldn't prove anything, he didn't have a case. The police officer then confessed that he hadn't seen any women in the area."

At that moment, I would have liked to kick both of those men below the belt, but there was nothing I could do. For that one day, we had been able to work our way out of the system, but we knew that there would be other days in which we wouldn't be so lucky.

When I got home that evening, my mother was waiting on the couch. I almost collapsed in her arms when I saw her. I explained what had happened, and I told her that it was all unfair. She pulled me into a great big hug and said, "I know, baby. I know." Then she started signing me a song. "We ain't gonna let nobody turn us around, turn us around, turn us around . . ." As her voice hummed softly in the quiet air, I slid in closer to her body. It was a song I had heard many times while we were out working in the cotton field. It was all about the hard times in life, how if we work hard we will eventually prevail, and things will get better. I never took those words to heart while I was in the field—there, they were just words to pass the time—but back here at home, and they felt real for the first time.

"Mom?" I said, "Why do we sing those songs if nothing's getting better?"

She pulled my head from her body and turned it so I could see her eyes. "Baby," she said, "Things are getting better. You may not see it because you're so young, but things are getting better." She paused for a moment, and let my head lay back on her shoulder. Then she said, "We've come a long way, but there's still a long road ahead of us. That's why we sing those songs, baby. They're there to inspire us, to give us hope, to give us something to hold onto." When she said that, she clenched her fist in mid-air, as if she were really holding onto something. "They call it soul music," she said, "It's meant to strengthen our soul, and give us all hope for a better tomorrow." At that moment, she started crying too. I could feel it against her chest. We stayed on the couch together, locked in each other's arms, just crying and singing songs long into the night.

Only a few weeks after that, I had another incident in which I was wronged. I was walking home from a friend's house on the other side of the neighborhood. My stomach was grumbling, but I couldn't wait to get home to eat. For once, I had a little bit of change in my pocket, so I decided I would treat myself to a burger at a local restaurant called Burger Chef. I had always heard that they made really good burgers, but my family and I had never had the luxury of eating out before.

I took a turn outside of the neighborhood and continued down to the Burger Chef a short way up the street. When I walked in the door, I was greeted by one of the waiters.

"How can I help you, young man?" He said.

"Well," I said, "I'm looking to get a burger."

He just laughed, and said, "I'm sorry, we're all full here. Maybe you should go around and try the back entrance."

"Full? What do you mean?" I motioned my hands to the dining room. Aside from an odd number of people, the place was completely empty. I turned back to the waiter, but he didn't seem to be moved by my argument. He simply pointed at the door through which I had just entered. On the window were the words White Entrance. Apparently, he wanted me to walk around to the back of the building and use the Black Entrance to the same restaurant that I was already in.

I felt sick to my stomach. I didn't want to eat anymore. I just turned away from the waiter, left the building and walked back home.

I realize that I could have chosen to fight it, but I wasn't in any position to be a trailblazer at that time. I was already in deep with the law, and I would continue to be for years afterward. In my youth, I was arrested more than twenty times for civil disobedience. In every one of those instances, the charges were along the lines of "unlawful thinking", or even "reckless eyeballing"—another makeshift law meant to fill the jail cells with black youngsters who were otherwise innocent.

It wasn't fair, but there was obviously nothing I could do about it other than stand by my principles. My mom was a huge encouragement to me. From that night after my first arrest, I believed her that things would get better. To me, it seemed there wasn't anywhere to go but up.

After that incident with the Burger Chef, I made a pact with myself. I promised that I would do my best to counter the racism passively. I promised myself that if I were ever to make enough money, I would open my own restaurant—one that would serve all of its customers equally.

Switching Gears

In the weeks after that, I tried to stay away from the neighborhood border whenever I could. It was still rare to see a cop car, but whenever I did, I would tuck my head down and keep to myself. I did the best I could not to display any attitude of "unlawful thinking".

But there wasn't a lot of time to wander the town after that, anyway. In the fall of that year, I began attending Richwood High School. I was excited to be at the high school level, but the transition was still a bit rough for me because it meant I had to leave Mr. Robinson behind. I didn't know any of the teachers at Richwood High School, so it felt like I was walking out into the unknown wilderness. I promised Mr. Robinson that I would be strong, and that I would keep using my skills for the good of all people.

The pigeon shuffle had to be put on hold, too. As the school year started, my schedule became full and I had to focus on my academics. But my entrepreneurial side was still intact—it was burning, in fact—and I knew I would find another outlet for business in the near future.

Richwood was one of the only two black high schools in Monroe. Carroll was the other. Neither school had a lot of money, but they both provided quality education, and they both had the top two football programs in Louisiana. In the 1960's alone, Richwood and Carroll combined for seven state championships. Even when the white teams were thrown into the mix, there was never any doubt that our two schools were the best.

The hard part for me was that I was always compared to my brother, Simon. Simon was a living legend back then. In his four year career, he made the varsity team every season, and he never lost a game.

My first year, of course, I did not make the varsity team. That was an impossible task that was only reserved for the gods of football. Instead, I was forced to stay on the bench as the equipment manager. My only job, aside from organizing all the gear, was to stand next to my brother and make him look bigger by comparison.

But the Richwood team was not successful by my brother's legs alone. The real reason was Coach Mackie Freeze. Coach Freeze was legendary in Monroe football lore. By the end of his thirteen year career, he amassed 119 wins against 29 losses and one tie, he won the state championship four times, and won the conference title eight times. But I remember Coach Freeze most of all as the toughest man in Louisiana. He would never be a coach today, because he'd be thrown in jail after one practice, but back then, I guess the parents really wanted us to be disciplined and God knows we needed it!

He used to carry a wooden board with him that he used for whipping his players. He called it "Poppa", and whenever you messed up a play, he'd tell you to "Come over and meet my friend Poppa." Legend had it that he forged Poppa himself after a player on his team asked to go to the bathroom. Coach got so mad that he ripped a tree out of the ground and used it to whip the shit out of him.

By my sophomore year, I made it onto the varsity team, but I might have just as well made it into boot camp. Practices were as long as Coach wanted them to go. Sometimes, if he was in a really bad mood, we would be out on the field until well after sundown. We would stay there all day, busting our butts in the hot Louisiana summer, but we would never get a water break because Coach didn't believe in water breaks. He thought that water made us weak—that if he let us have water, it would only make us want more water in the future. I don't see the logic in that, and I didn't then, but I never wanted to cross Coach Freeze when he had Poppa in his hand.

Hunting for Crawfish

Richwood, as I mentioned, had a fine education system, but only as far as it could afford. Compared to the schools across town, it was dirt poor and the words "separate but equal" carried no meaning. We all knew the white schools on the other side of town had it better than us, even if the government claimed otherwise. Regardless, we made do with what we could.

In my biology class, we had a unit on animal dissection. Of course, many of the students were excited because we had never dissected an animal before—with adult permission, anyway.

Each year, though, the school would run into a problem when this unit came up on the schedule. The problem was that the school didn't have the funding to provide any specimens to the students, so we were left to get our own. You read that right—we had to get our own specimens. The first unit was on crawfish, which meant we were required to find and bring our own crawfish to school. Nowadays, that seems like a cruel and archaic form of schooling—I don't know, maybe it really was cruel and archaic—but that's how things went, and nobody ever thought to question it.

But for most people, I learned, getting crawfish was a difficult endeavor. Students from years past complained that they were too hard to come across, or they themselves did not wish to jump into a stream and fish for the little critters. Some students would show up to school without a specimen at all, and the teachers would have no other option than to have them sit out for the activity. I thought this was unfair. It was unfair to the teachers and to the students, but most of all, in my eyes, it was incredibly unfair that nobody had ever thought to turn a profit from this situation.

The day that we received the assignment, I swear I had the blood of Mr. Robinson running through my veins. I didn't see any words on the assignment sheet; all I saw was opportunity. I gathered my friends after school. There were Don Zimmerman, Perry Thomas, Robert Pimpleton and David Washington—four of my most trusted friends. We met up behind the school building, which wasn't far from a stream that ran through the town.

"Gentlemen," I said, "There are many men and women out there that need us today. There is a shortage of crawfish in the community, but the demand is high. I've gathered you here because I know that each one of you possesses a gift—a gift of crawfish hunting." They all scoffed at my comments. Maybe I was being a little melodramatic, but behind the façade was the young man who had run the most successful pigeon shuffle in Louisiana history only two years earlier. They had no reason to doubt that I was all business.

We hit the trail and headed for the stream. It had rained the day before, which was good news for us, because it meant the crawfish were out and about. We got to the river and dropped in some buckets, then started hunting. It was a goldmine. There were crawfish everywhere—so many you had to be careful where you were stepping. We were out there for the rest of the afternoon, and by sundown we had gathered enough game to dole out to the entire student body of Richwood.

We kept the crawfish in giant buckets filled with water, and let them sit there overnight. When dawn broke, the guys and I rose early and carried the buckets to campus. As the students began arriving, we put on our business faces.

"Get your crawfish here! Crawfish here!" I yelled. Don was right beside me, yelling, "Fifteen cents for a crawfish, perfect for dissection, guaranteed to have the best organs in all of Louisiana!"

We made a killing in sales that morning. When we got to our biology period that afternoon, we saw that just about everyone was sporting an official Profit & Friends crawfish. Some of the girls had neglected to buy them, however, and complained to the teacher that we were selling them at a price that was far too high. Mr. Pierce, the science teacher, had a different view. He was big on free enterprise, and he told the girls that if they wanted the product I was selling, they would have to either catch their own or meet the price. It was a matter of supply and demand. The words rang through my brain as though

Mr. Robinson were there in the flesh. I realized that I really had dominated the market. I figured that if I could make it happen at a small high school in Monroe, then one day I could make it happen out in the real world. That was the first time I really felt motivated to make something of my name.

I almost forgot the best part—that day was the time I learned my lesson in business before pleasure. Before class, I had given a pair of free crawfish to a few young ladies I had had my eye on all year. It might have been an odd gift, but it seemed to catch their attention. When the guys found out about my backdoor escapade, they made sure I paid back in full, and then some.

A Lesson in Demonstration

Despite the school's financial troubles, I was able to have fun at Richwood High. I enjoyed my teachers, my classmates and my friends, and I wouldn't trade it for anything. What I've learned growing up in a poor neighborhood is that true happiness comes from our relationships. It comes from the people we care about, and the people who care about us. It doesn't matter where we are, or how much money we have. In the end, it's all about loving others and being loved. In Monroe, our hearts were full of love even if our wallets were empty. That's the only reason any of us prospered in that town. It was because of love.

By 1965, the world around us had escalated into a full-on war for civil rights. There were large protest marches in Selma and Montgomery, and smaller ones all across the South. Every day, news was coming out of some other southern town, dictating the story of a demonstrator who was killed, or a riot that was broken up by the police. The movement was gaining national attention, and even whites were joining in the fight. At the same time, it both excited and terrified me. It seemed that mom was right, that things were going to get better, but I never knew if or when Monroe, Louisiana would be next on the map.

For the most part, I had done a good job of staying out of trouble ever since my "reckless eyeballing and unlawful thinking" incident. I never treaded too close to any questionable areas. It wasn't that hard, because most of the things I wanted to do, and most of the things I cared about, were all in Bryant's Addition.

As I grew older, though, I yearned for a way to branch out into the greater world. I had seen what some of the protestors had done around the country. Some people refused to leave "whites only" restaurants, others refused to give up their seats on a bus. I figured I had as much of a right as any of them to go out into the battle field and fight, and I prayed for the day that I would make a successful stand against segregation.

Nevertheless, on the day that I finally made my stand, I learned the reason so few people were willing to do so. It was out of pure, unadulterated fear.

On that day, my friends Robert, Earnest, Titwell and I decided to go bowling at a local alley. It was a rare occasion for all of us, partly because money was tight and there wasn't a lot of room in the budget for bowling, but mostly because the only alley within walking distance straddled the line between the white and black neighborhoods.

The parking lot was deserted, save for a few cars near the side of the building. If not for the Open sign on the door, I would have thought the building was abandoned. I pushed the door open and entered into the dark, musty lobby. All I could smell was smoke and beer, and all I could see were a few run-down lanes with a group of white guys, not much older than us, at the last lane smoking cigarettes and drinking beer out of dirty glasses.

I turned to the front counter. The older gentleman behind the register was wiping a bowling shoe with a dirty rag. He peered up, saw us waiting, then turned back to his shoe and continued wiping.

"Excuse me, sir," I said. My dad always told me to call white people "Sir", no matter what they looked like. I didn't know the reason why, but I always trusted he knew what he was talking about.

Again, the man raised his head. He squinted his eyes, as if he couldn't make out a group of black kids in the dim lighting of the room. "What is it?" He spat.

"Well, my friends and I would like to bowl." I said it as though it was obvious, but he didn't seem to think so.

"Good," he said, "I hope you find an alley that lets your kind in, 'cause you ain't bowling here." Again, he turned back to his shoe and continued wiping it.

I could have dropped the issue. We could have left then and there. It had happened many times before; at stores, at restaurants, even at public bathrooms. There was no reason to fight the system. But then I thought of the demonstrators in Montgomery. I thought of Dr. King and his strong willpower. I saw myself in his shoes for one fleeting moment, and said, "Sir, the law says that you have to serve us just like you serve the white folks."

By then, the group of bowlers had taken notice and stopped bowling to watch the scene unfold. The man behind the counter nearly ripped the shoe he was holding in half. He stopped wiping, and then turned his full face to ours. The light was dim, but at that moment I could tell that the man was no longer white—he was beet red.

"Boy, the law ain't got shit on me. You think I'm going to give my business to a bunch of niggers? I'll call the cops right now. Whose side do you think they'll take?"

It was a bold threat. The memory of the court room flooded back into my brain: I remembered sitting in the handcuffs with the white judge and the white police officer. I knew right then that I had lost. "Come on, boys" I said, "Let's get out of here."

We left the building, then found the train tracks and followed them toward home. We never saw the man behind the counter again, but it wasn't long at all before the group of bowlers caught up with us. We heard their engine roaring from a mile away, and by the time their truck reached our side, the noise was so loud that we might as well have been looking at an oncoming train.

We tried to look the other way as we walked down the tracks, but they were too persistent. They followed the road that ran parallel to the tracks, taunting us with profanities and slurs. "Hey, look at the bunch of coons!" One of them shouted out the window. It was obvious they were all drunk. "Hey coons, don't you know bowling is a human sport?!" A stream of hoots and hollers followed behind. I turned my eyes only slightly, and I could see there were four of them in the truck. I quickly turned back to the path in front of me.

Tidwell, who was behind me, said as quietly as he could over the engine, "Let's get away from here. I don't like where this is headed."

"I don't either," I heard Robert say, "But home is that way. Anywhere else is just as bad as this. Maybe even worse." We all knew he was right, but nobody wanted this to continue.

I heard glass shatter, and I looked to my left. A beer bottle lay in pieces on the ground only inches from where Robert was standing. I looked to his face, then to the guys in the truck. I realized it was time to give up the act.

"What the hell was that for?" I shouted. I could barely hear myself over the engine, but they didn't seem to be paying attention anyway. I shouted louder, "We left the bowling alley! What else do you want?" My last words rang loud, because their engine cut off mid-sentence. I now saw that the truck was parked. My heart skipped a beat. Then, one by one, I saw them climb out of the nearside door.

I took a step back, almost tripping on a rail.

Ernest reiterated what I already tried to explain, "We don't mean no harm." His voice was quaking, but he went on, "We left the alley, just let us go home."

But his words didn't faze them. As their figures got closer, we saw them rise above us. They were bigger and meatier, and it was obvious we didn't stand a chance in a fight. They circled around all four of us, sealing away any hope of escape. The sun was low in the sky, and the air was beginning to get cold. I felt my legs trembling, and my entire body shivering. I tried to imagine home, deep in the warm arms of my mother, but the image quickly faded.

"You niggers trying to take over our turf?" One of them said. I couldn't tell which one, as I couldn't tell them apart anymore. The sun had cast a shadow across all of their faces, transforming each one into a dark silhouette.

Ernest tried to respond again, "We didn't mean—"He coughed out his next breath. I turned to see what had happened, and saw him lying on the ground, keeled over one of the rails. One of the men had kicked him in the gut. I saw the man reach into his back pocket and flip something into his hand. By the last glint of the sun I could tell what it was. Small, metal and sharp. The moment lasted an eternity. Everything was still. I could hear the beads of sweat trickle down from my forehead.

"You boys had better listen to what we say," the man said, "You're in our country."

I felt an arm on my wrist. Each one of them grabbed one of us and dragged us to their truck. They threw us in the back bed, and two of them stayed in back to guard us. The driver hopped in, turned the truck around and started heading out of town.

I remember riding for miles, sitting in the back bed in a terribly uncomfortable position, but too afraid to make any move. Every time the truck hit a bump in the road, I winced in pain. I just stared down at my hands in my lap, too afraid to look anywhere else. I noticed how my hands were together, as if I were wearing handcuffs riding to court once again, but this court felt even more crooked than the last one.

I then began to see my hands in a different way. I noticed they were folded together, just liked they were when I went to church. I took it as a sign, and began to pray.

Lord, I prayed, if they kill us tonight, please look after my family. Let them know that I'm okay, and let them be okay. Please let them grow. Let my daddy live to see better days than this. Lord, please. Lord, please.

I kept repeating that phrase quietly to myself. It was my last thread, the only thing I had to hold onto.

The truck turned onto a private dirt road. Now we were in the middle of the country, on a farm, it appeared, and the sun was well below the horizon. The truck rumbled to a stop just in front of a big red barn. The driver killed the engine and hopped out of his door. The passenger hopped out of his, then went to the barn and slid open the large door at the front. Through the door, I saw nothing but pitch darkness. It scared me in a way that I had never been scared before—like I was staring through the gates of hell.

One of the men yanked at my collar and told me to get out of the truck. One by one, they led us into the barn with our heads down and lined us up at the back wall. After a moment of standing in pitch darkness, somebody lit a lantern, and I could see three sets of quivering feet beside mine. All four of us were crying, but I didn't dare look up to see their faces.

Finally, one of them spoke, "What are we gonna do with you niggers? You can't seem to stay on your own side of town."

"You can't stop us from going nowhere. You can't stop us from going bowling." One of my friends spoke. I couldn't tell which one it was, but he could barely finish the last word, he was shaking so hard.

The man was surprised that one of us had been so bold. He was quick to respond, but he drew out his words, as though he was preparing for something. He said, "Boy . . . I can make you do anything I want to." There was silence for a moment, and then I heard a terrible sound—a sound that still frightens me to this day.

Click.

At the sound of the gun chamber, loaded and cocked, I didn't know if my heart would ever beat again. Mostly, I was afraid for whichever one of us had spoken. Now he was first on the list.

"Please, sir!" I shouted. Now I was weeping, and my words spilled through my tears. My head was bowed against the wall. I couldn't see anything, but I felt their presence. I felt everything in the entire room. "Please, sir," I repeated, "Don't shoot us."

But the man only laughed. "Sir?" He mimicked, "You calling me sir? Are you kidding me, boy? You think your manners will save you now?"

I didn't think any of that. I thought back to what my dad had said, about being polite to the white people. I guess it was my last stand. A tribute to my father. A symbol that I had stayed true to the end.

I heard another voice, scared and trembling, but it wasn't one of ours. "Hey, come on, man. Put the gun down. We scared 'em enough." He was clearly drunk, just like all the others.

"I ain't putting no gun down!" The man shouted. His voice was frantic, his words shaking. My heart accelerated with each word he spoke. "I'm sick of these niggers wandering the streets like they run the town! It's time someone put an end to it!"

"Oh come on! They're just kids! They ain't starting no trouble!" There was a pause. For a moment I heard nothing. The whole world stood still. For all I knew, there was no longer a world outside the walls of the barn. I closed my eyes tight and said a quick prayer.

Click.

My body shook at the sound, but nothing came after. I kept my eyes closed and waited it out. Still, nothing.

Finally, the man with the gun spoke once more, softly, but sternly. "Alright. You niggers get out of here and don't look back. If you do, you've got a bullet waiting for you."

I flipped my eyes open. I exhaled, and then quickly drew in a large breath of air. It tasted sweet. For the first time in my life, I was thankful to be able to breathe. All four of us stood there, not knowing what to do. We kept our heads still pressed against the wall, waiting for any indication that it was all a cruel joke. Finally, he said his last words. "And if you know what's right for you, you'll stay on your side of town with the rest of yah."

Carefully, I picked my head up. At any moment I was ready to die, but it didn't come. I was still there, and so were my friends. I turned away from the wall, but I still kept my eyes away from stares of the other men. I couldn't bear to look at them. I slowly brought a hand to my face and wiped away a pool of tears. Through the enduring quiver in my voice, I spoke the first words of the rest of my life. They were the same words I had said earlier in the day at the bowling alley, "Come on, boys. Let's get out of here."

When I first began to process the whole incident on the long walk home that night, I realized that those men had no reason not to kill us. Like the man at the bowling alley said, the law was not on our side. They had no reason not to shoot us there on the spot and bury us in the field. The only thing that could have changed their minds was the spirit of the Lord.

When I got home that night, I didn't want to say a word about anything that had happened. I didn't want my parents to know that I had been in danger. But that was often the case, they read me like a book.

"Joe, where have you been?" my dad said, "What's wrong?"

But I didn't say anything. Before I could eke out a word, my face clenched tight, and I let the tears stream down my face. My dad came to me and pulled me into a hug.

"It's okay, my boy," he said, "It's okay. It's okay."

"Dad?" I said, piecing the word together through my tears.

"Yes?"

"Why do you tell us to respect the white men?"

My dad choked on his words. He didn't even know what happened, but he could tell it was something big. "Well, Joe, I tell you that, first, because it's the right thing to do, and second, because it's the only way they'll come around. If we treat them like dirt, then they have reason to treat us like dirt too, but if we treat them like kings, well, then we just might get a little bit better than dirt in return."

At first, I wasn't sure at first if I wanted to include this story in my book. It was hard for me to start writing. But eventually I realized that that's what makes it so powerful, and so close to my heart. I believe it's a story that needs to be told, not to scold the men that treated us wrong, but to demonstrate how far we've come since then.

That night was the scariest night of my life, but it reminded me that the Lord was by my side. After that night, I was able to trust that He had a plan for everyone. I was able to trust that He knew what He was doing, and that things would eventually get better. From then on, I had a heart for change. I didn't want to be a bystander in life any longer; I wanted to be the one who made the difference for others. The Lord showed me that night that there was a reason He kept me alive, and in response, I decided I would do whatever it takes to follow through on His plan.

4 Four

THE POWER OF EXPECTATIONS

The Power of Expectation

I like to think of people as very malleable beings. A lot of the things we do in our lives are reactions to the world around us. Think of it this way: The fact that you're reading this book right now means that you've reacted to many of society's constructions. 1) You or someone you know has purchased this book. This means that you've accepted society's monetary system. 2) You've learned to read. You or your elders saw that it was important for you to be a reading citizen in a society that almost demands literacy. The list goes on, but the point of it all is simple. You react and conform to the expectations of your society. There would be no expectation for you to earn dollars and cents if you lived in a world without a monetary system. There would be no expectation for you to be literate in a world with no written language.

This is the power of expectation. We mold to our society's expectations without even knowing it. That was the true power of the neighborhood in which I was raised. Even though the rest of the world cast off Bryant's Addition as just another poor black neighborhood out of the thousands of others, we didn't listen. We knew we were special. As a community, we built each other up. Our parents raised us to aim high and never stop improving.

However, when I think of all the children in my situation who were not so lucky, I feel remorse. Society wants them to believe that they are inferior, so they start believing it themselves. The truth is that they are the same as anyone else. The only things inferior about them are the expectations in which they are raised. Low expectations make us believe that we're not good enough to aim high, and that we are not meant for greatness. Low expectations are a disease, and once they fester inside of a community, they spread into the hearts of everyone born thereafter. It creates a cycle that can last for generations.

I was blessed that my parents and my community had high expectations. That was the special ingredient. That was the "stuff in the water" that nobody on the outside could see. When we, the youth living in Bryant's Addition, learned that we were expected to aim high, there was only one option. Aim high.

The Power of Expectation on the Football Field

By the time I was a junior in high school, our team had become the biggest thing in town—and I was the starting running back. Collectively, the team had strung together over 40 wins and two state titles, and as the streak grew longer, the expectation that we would win grew higher. It got to the point that winning was no longer a celebratory occasion—rather, it was the food for an addiction.

Each week, our opponents would cower further and further in fear. Their knees would quake as they heard our cleats stomping onto the field, waiting to be trampled by a stampede.

Midway through the season, we were facing Morehouse High School in Bastrop, Louisiana. It was a game I'll remember forever because it taught me a lesson on the power of expectation. Like the other schools, Morehouse was expected to lose in a landslide. To us, their name looked less like a foe and more like another check mark on our schedule.

But during the first half of the game, they proved that they were more than that. They played us tough, and painted the field in our fumbles, bad blocks and missed tackles. Each play proved more agonizing to watch than the last. By halftime, we found ourselves crouched over in the locker room, sickened by our poor play. The score was 26-0 in their favor.

Coach Freeze stood at the center of the huddled players and shouted, "You're embarrassing yourselves, boys! You don't look like you're trying to pummel those guys into the ground. You look like you're trying to sell them cookies at a bake sale!"

It was obvious that he was unprepared for this speech—nobody, even him, thought we would be in this position. His anger exposed a vein in his forehead we had never seen before, and the words flew out of his mouth with fury.

"I don't know about you, but I came here to win! The problem is all you boys thought it would come easy! Thought if we got enough wins, they'd give us one free! Well, this isn't a damn coffee shop, this is football! You've got to earn each win!"

Nobody spoke. The last of his words echoed off the lockers and sunk into silence. Now I could hear the breathing of everyone around me. We were out of sync, and it didn't seem like anyone was in the mood to get back in sync.

Coach kept the anger pasted across his face. "I know what the problem is," he said, "You came onto this field having not lost a game in three years. Right? You knew you were going to win. Right?" He raised his hand to point toward the other team's locker room, "But apparently they didn't read the memo that they were supposed to lose!"

I looked up, and so did a few of my teammates. None of us had any idea where he was going. He cleared his throat as he saw more faces turn his direction. Then, he heaved in a breath and said, "You see, boys . . . these big dumbasses can't read!"

The locker room burst open in laughter. Coach's angry face softened up a little bit, but he wasn't smiling just yet, "We need to go out there and show them who's supposed to win! We need to go teach these dumbasses how to read!"

We all shouted in unison. The heads of my teammates were no longer hanging low. They were all gazing upward just as we should have been the whole time. At that moment, we became electrified, and the energy flowed between each one of our players. We became one.

In the second half, we not only taught them to read, but we taught them a simple lesson in arithmetic: 27 is greater than 26. We left the field that night as one-point victors, and we learned what kind of power could be unleashed if we only raised our expectations. We were reminded that we were capable of success, even if the whole world begged to differ.

That's the lesson I like to teach people about the power of expectation. It seems that expectation is half the battle. Every once in a while, if we're not reminded of our own capabilities, we can begin to slump, lie down on the field and let the lies of the outside world take over. But it doesn't have to be this way. You and I are meant for success. Just like my team in the locker room, we need to be reminded of our capabilities. As long as we know what we're truly capable of, we can overcome the lies of the world. We can remember that we are supposed to win.

Once we had the mentality that we were supposed to win, winning became even easier. We extended our winning streak further, and a lot of those wins were attributed to Coach Freeze's raised expectations.

Along with the winning streak, a lot more fanfare came to the Richwood football team. Anyone who knows southern football knows that the high school team is the most important, most anticipated and most exciting part of any community. But this winning streak made that sense of community explode from a pastime to an obsession. Each week as the streak grew longer, there was even more pressure to win. The school felt the pressure, my teammates and I felt the pressure, and my coaches felt the pressure.

Coach Freeze was well-aware of his burden that he carried. Not only did he hold us to a high standard, but he was held to an even higher standard by the community. He had to win, or else it would be his head on trial for the whole week to come.

Even with that pressure, though, I admire Coach Freeze for sticking to his principles. He was tough, for sure, but he was a man of integrity, and he held that integrity to a higher regard than any of his statistical accomplishments. I remember the policy he had in place for his players. He mandated that we each maintain a GPA that was higher than the school average. If we didn't, it was goodbye to the team. At first, it seemed easy enough—all we had to do was stay in the 50th percentile. But there was a problem we figured out right away. We realized that there were dozens of students on the team, so if each of them was trying to make the grade that meant the school's GPA would climb higher as well. I reckon Coach Freeze knew this, I also reckon he didn't give a care in the world.

I remember that I never had the greatest grades in high school. I was good, but not great. Not to the standard that I should have been. But because of Coach Freeze's incredibly high expectations for us, I and a lot of other players started trying harder off the field. The embarrassment of being cut from the football team was reason enough to get ourselves in line. And guess what? It worked! My teammates and I started getting better grades.

It was the same principle that Coach used in the locker room. If we knew what we were worth, then there was no reason for us to give half the effort.

Coach Freeze always said that his biggest accomplishment was when the team's quarterback was named valedictorian in the consecutive seasons. It was this kind of character that made him loved by the community, even though at times, he was feared by his players. I'll remember Coach Freeze for motivating me, and I'll remember him for standing up for his principles—that the education is more important than the sport. I took these principles from my high school football years, and still keep them with me today. Coach Freeze made a positive impact in my life and in the lives of countless other men all because he chose not to take the easy way out. My only hope is that the community remembers him for his integrity as much as his coaching record.

The First Loss

Late in my senior season, we did eventually lose a game. Peabody High School from Alexandria, Louisiana trampled over us with a score of 34-7, ending our streak at 66 games. After the game, we were all shocked. We had never faced a team even near that caliber of maturity and size. They were growing full length beards while we were still learning to use razors. It had felt like their men were from a different level of play altogether. Most of all, I felt ashamed because we had let the winning streak slip away on our watch. After the game was over, we treaded off the field with our 'tails between our legs.' We felt like we had failed for the first time. Nonetheless back in the locker room, Coach dispelled our feelings of shame.

"All streaks have to come to an end. Records are made to be broken," he said. He looked us all directly in the eyes, even though we could see an obvious pain in his. Nobody really wanted to say anything after that game, but Coach knew he couldn't waver. He continued, "I'm proud of you men. I truly mean that. During this stretch of games, you've shown the town, the school and yourselves what you can accomplish as a team."

He could see the somber look on our faces as well. It was as if a black hole had sucked all the air out of the room. He took a glance around until he found a football on a bench. He picked it up and held it out for everyone to see.

"Football is a way of life," He said. "You guys know that more than anyone else in this town. Some of you have lived and breathed football here for the past four seasons. But in life, as well as in football, you're going to run into roadblocks along the way. Even when you're the best in the game—when you're one top of the world, that just means there are a million other people reaching and grabbing at you, trying to bring you back down."

He brought the football back down to his side, and then his voice softened until it was almost a whisper. Together as a team, we all leaned forward to try to hear him. Maybe there was no air in there, because it got so quiet I don't think anyone was breathing. He said, "But don't let anyone bring you down. If you run into a roadblock, you've got two options. You can run away, or you can . . . what? Joe?"

My heart skipped a beat. His eyes and the football were pointing right at me. My throat quaked as I scrambled for an answer, "You can run away, or you can plow through them." I liked my answer. It seemed to go right along with my inclination toward the running back position.

Until coach said, "Wrong."

My heart skipped another beat. I didn't like being dangled out in front of the whole team like that, let alone after our first loss. But coach gave me the reprieve. He turned back to the team, held the ball tight to his chest and said, "When you run into a road block, you stare it straight in the face. You tell it that you're not going to be swayed, cause you're stronger than that roadblock. You make sure it's watching as you place your foot on its face and turn it into a stepping stone."

The room stayed silent. I didn't understand it at first, so I raised my hand.

"Yes, Joe?"

"But Coach . . . walking over it. Isn't that the same as plowing straight through it?" I flinched backward, ready for a verbal beating in front of all of my teammates. But Coach didn't lash out at me. He actually seemed pleased.

"Joe, when you run through something, you're still at ground level. When you make it your stepping stone, you can use it to catapult you upward. You see, we learn from our drawbacks. We learn from the roadblocks in life. We don't ignore them. We use them to make ourselves better. So then the question becomes, 'How are we going to learn from this?'" After he said that, he stood down and walked out of the locker room, taking the football with him.

At that moment, all the air seemed to flow back into our bodies, and we breathed a breath in unison. In the following weeks, our team became stronger where our weaknesses had been exposed. We went on to win each game the rest of the season.

After the season ended, it was discovered that Peabody had brought back some of their former players from college in order to beat us, and they were ruled ineligible by the state Governing Board. So even though we were dealt our first loss, we found out later that it was really a win. We were all excited to hear the news, but Coach Freeze was less enthusiastic. He felt that if we were really the champions of the league, then we could have taken on the team no matter what. He declined to accept the championship by default, saying that it was not the right thing to do. The following year, the team won an undisputed state title.

STEPPING OVER THE LINE

The Power of Integrity

With graduation on the horizon, the issue of choosing a college eventually drew nearer, and I was reminded of my expectations. For me, there had always been two expectations that stemmed from the outside world. The first was that I was expected to attend college and graduate. My parents had made this clear to me and my siblings our entire childhood. They didn't want me settling for less like so many of the other youth around me, and at that time the only other option was leaving to fight in the Vietnam War. I had seen the war take many of our young people in my neighborhood away from home, and my parents did not want to see me have the same fate. Even though college was expensive and money was sparse, they had decided long before that my future would be more important than theirs.

The second expectation was that I would go to either Grambling State University or Southern University—both of which were historically black universities in my area. In fact, each one of the college-bound teammates from my graduating class would choose either Grambling or Southern, and that came as no surprise to anyone. Of course, I had considered both of these schools, but as I pondered my options, I realized that this expectation of me was unfair. I didn't want to go with the grain just to go with the grain.

Earlier in the year, I had laid out three goals for myself, and I had decided that the school I chose had to have the accommodations for all three of them; 1) Graduate in four years and make the dean's list, 2) Play football in the fall, and 3) Run track in the spring. While Grambling and Southern were certainly capable of providing me with these opportunities, I needed to find the place that would best allow me to achieve them.

During the summer, I was given the opportunity to work out with the team at Alcorn State in Mississippi. The school appealed to me most of all, because it was where Mr. Robinson had gotten his accounting degree. He was one of the only black businessmen in Monroe. All other graduates were either strictly teachers or blue collar workers. I loved nearly all of my teachers, but I didn't see myself going down that path.

Best of all, Alcorn had offered me a full scholarship if I chose to attend their school. It was an offer that my family and I couldn't refuse, given our financial situation. During the summer, I moved to the campus for my first week of training camp. That first week was an important time, because the team got to see me in action, but I also got to see them in action—that is, their university—to see if they met the criteria for my goals. I remember being shown into my dorm room the first day, and that proved to be the first sign of trouble. What little I was able to see through the dirty brown window didn't please the eye, and it was made worse by the stale smell that came from the furniture. When I set my bags down on the bed, I thought they might fall right through the mattress, and I was scared to think what I might do to it if

I tried to lie down. Over in the corner was a rickety old desk that looked like it was teetering on one leg. I knew I still had school work to take care of, and I would need to study every night, but I couldn't see myself doing well in a desk like that.

The worst part I remember, though, was the heat.

Now, we southern boys know heat. In the cotton fields, I was forced to make friends with the sun, but this was beyond what I had ever known. The heat seemed to be emanating from the walls, like they were coils in an oven, and opening the window did nothing to help. I was already preparing for my classes for the fall term, and I told my coach the first day that it was so hot in my room that I couldn't study, and that I had to study if I was going to play on the team. He told me not to worry, and that he'd get a box fan for my window. Of course, we didn't have air conditioning back then, so it was the best he could do, and I told him that that would be fine.

In the ensuing days at practice, it felt like the sun was no longer my friend; it was conspiring against me. At that time, we were doing three-a-day practices, and although I made a good impression on the field, I was completely drained by the end of each day. When I went back to my room at night, I found that it was still too hot to study. My coach still hadn't gotten me a box fan like he had promised, so I didn't have any way to get my schoolwork done.

I began to think about my goals. The first thing on the list, above all, was that I would go to college and graduate on the dean's list. I knew that if I were to stay at Alcorn in those conditions, I wouldn't be able to do that. Then I began to think about my options. Alcorn was planning on offering me a scholarship, and I knew that if I gave that up, it would be throwing away a golden opportunity. My parents had worked hard but didn't have enough money to send all of their children to school, so a scholarship was a special thing.

I decided to go to my coach the next day. We had been in practice for about two weeks and I still hadn't gotten the fan, so I asked him if he would please help me out. Again, he said he would, and even promised me he'd have the fan that night. At that point, I was already starting to question whether I could trust him, and I figured that this was the final straw. When I went back to my room that night, I found that the fan still hadn't come. I looked around at the vacant, crusty old room and decided enough was enough. I threw my things in my foot locker, got a ride over to the Centennial bus station and headed out of town.

During the ride, my hands were shaking so much I'm surprised I didn't rip the handle off my suitcase. Not only was I angry at my coach, but I was scared, because I knew what waited for me back in Monroe. I still had no plan, and I didn't know how anyone would react—other than angry. When I saw the sign that said Monroe was only a few miles away, I even considered just keeping myself on board, passing up the town and riding to some unknown destination. It didn't seem like that much worse of a fate.

But something in the town was calling me home. It tugged at my heart and eventually, when we got to the stop, it pulled me off the bus. I called one of my friends to pick me up and take me home.

When I got home, I walked into the door and dropped my bags on the floor. I saw that the kitchen light was still on, so I walked in. There at the table was my dad. His eyes told the whole story, and I knew his words before he even spoke.

"Son, what are you doing back here?"

I swallowed, but my throat was dry, like I hadn't taken a drink of water in days. "Dad," I said through a croak in my voice, "I needed to come home."

"You walked away from a scholarship?" He said. There were years of hard work in the wrinkles on his face, and I couldn't bear to look at him. I glanced around the room, at the old, crusty walls of the kitchen, the chipped countertop, and the shaky table that stood on the concrete floor where my dad was sitting. At that moment, I felt like the worst son in the world. But I still felt, beneath it all, that I was right.

"Dad," I started, "I couldn't study there. The coach said he'd get me a fan to help with the heat, but he never did."

"You walked away from a scholarship because you didn't have a fan? Son, we don't even have a fan here!"

I stood my ground. It was never about the fan. I knew it was about something else. I took a deep breath, and then said, "Dad, the fan doesn't matter. My coach lied to me, and I can't play for a coach that's going to lie to me."

The moments that followed my words felt more like an empty space, a vacancy where nothing else existed, and I couldn't for the life of me decide what to do. Finally, my dad filled the vacancy. He leaned forward and put his elbows on the table. He rubbed his forehead, then turned back to meet me. This time, I looked him in straight the eyes and didn't waver.

"Well," he said, "Sit down . . . Let's figure out what you're going to do now."

Choosing Northeast

I don't know if I slept at all that night. My dad and I stayed in the kitchen well into the morning, laying all of my options out on the table. The biggest concern, we both knew, was that I had to pay for my school now. We were scraping pennies as it was, but if I couldn't afford my tuition, it meant that I would have to go fight in the war. I knew my parents didn't want that for me, but that only meant that they'd have to drain more of their own money to keep me from going. I hated that idea. It kept biting at me the whole time we were there, and I managed to eke out an apology whenever I could get up the courage.

"Dad, I'm sorry. I know it wasn't the smartest decision to leave." That's all I could say. What else was there to say when we both knew it was true?

He just kept his eye on the papers in front of him, and said, "What's done is done, son. There's no looking back, just looking forward."

There's no looking back, just looking forward. I thought about that for a long time that night. Even when my dad had gone to bed and we hadn't gotten any further, I stayed awake in my bed—the bed I'd grown up in and grown out of. I thought more about money—we didn't have any. I thought about the color of my skin—I had the short end of the stick there too. I realized that for a kid like me, there wasn't a whole lot I could look back on because I was at the back of the line, but there was a whole world of progress that I could make.

The next morning, as each of my younger siblings and my mother got up and saw with a puzzled look that I was there too, I was reminded again and again of the audacious decision that I had only made a few hours earlier. After breakfast, the kitchen was left again to just me and my dad. My heart had been thumping the whole morning, waiting for this moment, not knowing what to expect. He started putting the dirty dishes in the sink.

"Well," he said, "Have you thought it over?"

"Yes sir."

"And have you made a decision?"

"Yes sir."

"So, you're going to go to Grambling?"

This was the moment. It felt the same as when I had gotten home last night, eager just to get it done with, to see his reaction. "No sir," I said, "I'm going to go try out for Northeast."

The bowl he was scrubbing fell into the sink, and I winced at the sound that clamored off the walls, leaving the room in silence. He just turned to me and didn't say anything. His face was scrunched up, like I had just made a joke that wasn't funny.

Again, I understood what he was thinking even though he didn't speak. There was no question about the gravity of what I had just said. Northeast was the university on the other side of Monroe—the white side. It was simply out of the question—I might as well have told him I wanted to go join the girl scouts.

I kept my face firm, though, eyes looking straight at him to let him know that I was serious. I continued, "I want to take Coach Abe . Pierce, III down there with me and talk to the football coach. I want to try out for their team." Coach Pierce was my track coach, and other than Mr. Robinson, he was the only person I knew who felt confident around white men.

Finally my dad found his voice again. "Son," he said, "Northeast . . . that's a white school."

"I know that, sir."

"Well, why do you want to go to a white school? That doesn't make any sense."

"Maybe not, but you remember what you said last night about looking forward?" He nodded. "Well, I thought it over, and I know this is the right thing to do. This is moving forward. For all of us."

My dad looked back into the sink, as if he was going to find an answer somewhere down the drain. He knew that when I said all of us, it meant more than just the family. Finally, he picked up the bowl he had dropped and started scrubbing it again. He slowly shook his head, then said, "Son, do what you gotta do. Things aren't going to get any better if nobody does anything."

Meeting Coach Dixie B.White

To tell you the truth, there wasn't a whole lot of hope in my heart. I sat staring out the window of my high school track coach's truck as we rumbled down the road toward Northeast. I didn't know what to expect, mainly because I had never even been to the campus in my life—in fact, I would have been hard pressed to tell you where it was.

Coach Pierce came with me to help convince the coach that I was worthy of being on the team, though I figured he was just as nervous as I was that day. On top of the fact that I figured I'd be the only black athlete—or even the only black student—at Northeast, I first had to prove that I could make it at the school. I didn't have a scholarship and my GPA was well below my time in the 40-yard dash, so there wasn't a lot working in my favor this time around.

My whole life I had always felt like a big guy. Even on the football team in high school, a lot of my friends were thinner, and weaker than me. But as the truck rounded the corner to the practice field that day, it made me realize that being big and feeling big are two different things. Northeast was in training camp just like Alcorn, and out on the field I could see a whole lot of white players running drills. A lot of them were smaller than me, too, but as the truck got closer, I started to feel really small. I leaned backward as if I could sink right into my seat. That's the first time I got a taste for what I was embarking upon.

Luckily, the minute we pulled in, I heard the coach blow his whistle, and everyone on the field gathered into a huddle. He seemed to be giving them a pep talk. I heard his voice crescendo a number of times, and none of the words were all too friendly. A few moments later, he broke the group apart and the players started heading for the locker room.

I looked at my coach. "Ready?" he asked.

I nodded, though I wasn't feeling it... We both got out of the car and walked over to the table where some of the coaches and equipment managers were gathering. A few of them were chatting to each other, pointing at clipboards and drawing out plays, but when one of them saw us walking in their direction, the rest turned around to see the sight.

"Can I help you gentlemen?" A thin man with sun glasses and a baseball cap asked. It was the same man who had blown the whistle. I couldn't tell if his tone was truly curious or if it was condescending. He didn't look like the type who would take kindly to a couple of black guys on the field.

"Are you the head coach?" asked Coach Pierce.

The man smiled. "Dixie White," he said. My eyes widened. To me it sounded more like the name of a Klan group than the name of a person. I wondered what his parents were like, to name a child like that, but I didn't dare to ask him at the moment.

"Abe Pierce," my coach said, and the two of them shook hands. Then I offered mine and said, "Joe Profit."

"Well, what can I do for you men?"

"Joe here is looking for a place to play football this fall."

"Hah," he laughed, "for who?"

"For you, sir," he said.

He smirked, and spoke between his teeth, "No kidding . . . ". I had never before felt the way I felt then. Coach Dixie White was looking me over like I was some kind of show dog, as if he were going to ask me to sit, stay and roll over. His sunglasses prevented me from seeing his eyes, which made it a lot worse. After a good minute that left me sweating under the sun, he finally spoke, "You understand, son, that this here is a white school."

That was a little bit more candid than I had expected. "Yes, sir," I said. My politeness seemed to shock him. He pulled his sunglasses down the bridge of his nose, and for the first time I saw his eyes. "You trying to prove something here, son?"

"No, sir," I said, "All I want is a place to play football, run track and get a good education."

"A good education?" "Yes, sir. My goal is to graduate in four years and make the dean's list." This made coach laugh so loud, his voice echoed off of the nearby buildings. Looking back, I'm sure he must have felt like he was being pranked. In a matter of minutes he'd seen it all. "Son," he said, "I treat all my players the same, but you'd fighting an uphill battle. Even the white kids don't graduate in four years. Freshmen get redshirted and sit out their first year. You'd be lucky if you made it that far."

Even as the cynicism shone through his face, I stood my ground because I knew that I could do it. When he saw the sincerity in my face, he laughed again, "Well, son, you just might do it with that attitude. So tell me about yourself. What are you doing up here at Northeast instead of Grambling or Southern?"

I went on to explain my story about Alcorn State, how I had a full scholarship but walked away because I couldn't take it there anymore, because the coach kept lying to me.

"Well, son, I'm a man who's honest with my players, and if honesty is what you want, then let me be frank. The law says I gotta let everyone have a chance on my team, so if you want a tryout, I'll give you a tryout. But don't expect any favors out here." He pointed to the locker room, "You're gonna get killed by those guys if you join my team. Now that's just me being honest. And when that happens, I won't be there to peel you up off the turf, you understand?"

I nodded. "Yes sir."

Coach White smiled, "Well then . . . let's see what you got."

Team Vibe

From my graduating high school class, there were 12 of us who went on to play college football. Of those 12 athletes, 11 went to either Grambling or Southern. There was only one that went to a historically white university. In fact, there was only one black person in the entire South who played football for a historically white university—and that was me.

Making the decision to go to Northeast was never racially driven, though. It was not one of my ambitions to be a racial pioneer, and it was not one of my three goals of college. With that said, though, I was naïve to think that race would not play a huge role in my college career. I had no idea what the school had lying ahead for me. It wasn't until I got acclimatized to my daily life that I realized how right Coach White had been—I was in for an uphill battle.

I remember Coach White leading me onto the practice field my first day there. The sun was beating down, and everything was bright except for the tone of my skin. There were a dozen or so groups of friends chatting with one another, but once I came into view I began to draw stares and whispers from everyone. Undoubtedly, they figured some wanderer from Southern had lost his way. The whispers followed me over to the sideline, where Coach started explaining the routine. I nodded and pretended to listen to what he was saying, but it was hard to take my mind off the dozens of eyes peering over his shoulder. They reminded me of the men at the bowling alley. My hands began shaking and my heart began punching against the inside of my chest pad. The sun shone through my jersey and pulled out the buckets of sweat underneath.

Then Coach finished. "Any questions?"

I was startled by the question. I could have told him I hadn't been listening and that I had a whole list of questions to go over with him, but with the whole team staring me down, it didn't seem like the right time to make myself look stupid. I shook my head no.

"Well, then. Get out there and join the others." He patted me on the back and sent me toward the field. Until then, I had never experienced such an overwhelming feeling as I trotted out to meet my new teammates. I knew I was getting closer, but it was slow, like in a dream. I knew my legs were propelling me forward, but I couldn't feel them hitting the ground at all. It was all just one, fluid motion as my eyes met theirs for the very first time. The air between them was saturated in anger, and I didn't know why, but I felt it too.

Fight to the Finish

I took the ball from the quarterback, Steve Mansur. Over to the left, I saw the line was heavily under pressure, so I cut back right. A gap appeared between the guard and tackle. Green turf was all I saw ahead of me. As soon as I took off, my feet again seemed to float as I ran. The more I accelerated, the more I became liberated from the ground. A few moments later, I realized that it wasn't just my imagination. I found myself flying through the air. My head was jarred sideways, and my body hadn't even had a split second to feel the pain of the linebacker's helmet against my ribcage before I collided with the turf that looked so promising only a few moments earlier.

My head hung from my shoulder, and through my left ear hole I heard the call one more time, "Take that, nigger!" The linebacker stood tall like a hunter over his trophy, grinning widely as he straddled my twisted body.

I had heard that word many times before. Those days in Louisiana, you couldn't leave the comfort of your neighborhood without being reminded of it. But never had I heard the word so densely used than in the first few weeks of practice. It seemed like each time my body collided with the dirt, there was somebody waiting to add insult to injury. They always had that same smirk on their face, too, and after a while they didn't even seem to notice me when they said it. They looked to their friends, rather, like it was some type of social trend that they did to fit in. I felt like my teammates were all inside this circle, and I was a stray on the outside looking in.

This time I looked up and saw the man's face. No, I take that back—he wasn't a man at all. He was a boy. By the light of the sun gleaming off his shining white teeth, I saw the insecurity in his smile, and suddenly I became the hunter and he became the trophy. His leg was inches from my left hand. I snagged it, and then I pulled and brought him to the ground before his lips had time to seal away that pompous smile.

I pulled myself over his body and straddled him on my knees. I clenched my left fist around his jersey, pulled him to my face, and then gave him a look from hell. I saw the fear in his eyes as he squirmed beneath me, but I did not give in. I figured he had had his time for mercy. Everyone had. Now it was time for payback. I wound my right fist back then threw it forward into his fragile gut. He let out a loud, piercing wail, but it was cut short, silenced by my next blow. Over and over I threw all my rage into this one man who had driven me over the edge. I would have found a time to stop, but the man's eyes were filled with so much hatred that the sun could no longer reflect off the vacancy in his dark black pupils.

I raised another hand high in the air to give one last blow, but someone caught hold of my wrist. It was Coach White. Then another player took my other arm, and together they dragged me off the linebacker and threw me to the ground.

"Jesus, boy, what the hell is your problem?!" Coach yelled at me.

"Get the gorilla off the field!" Someone shouted.

I closed my eyes and tried to block it all out, but I couldn't. The sun was pouring down through my eyelids, and the world outside them was still there. All I wanted was to lunge back onto someone—anyone—and start throwing more punches. I felt pride and shame at the same time.

That wasn't the only time it happened, either. As the days went on, it started to become a routine. I would run, get tackled, get insulted, then let it all break loose. People began to fear me. Not in a healthy, competitive way, but in a way where they truly feared for their bodies. I was the only enemy on the team, and I was bringing everyone down because of it. One day, Coach White wanted to address the situation, so he took me into his office.

"Boy, I don't know what we're gonna do with you," he said, "You tell me to give you a shot on the team, and I give it to you. Now every day you're out there fighting some other guy. What do you expect me to think?"

I sat in the chair across from his desk, just staring down at my hands folded in my lap. I seriously thought at that moment that Coach was going to kick me off the team. I was already planning out how I would tell dad when I got home.

Coach continued, "Joe, I want you on my team because you can play football. That's all I ever cared about here. As long as you can do that, I don't give a damn about anything else. But if you keep starting fights like this, then you're distracting the players, and I can't have that on my football team." Coach was brutally honest. At times he'd treat me like garbage, and he sounded like he hated me, but the truth was that Coach treated all his players like garbage. It was a sort of affectionate garbage. He only saw our potential for football, and I guess for the sake of the team that was a good thing. "So what's it going to be, then?"

I said, "Coach, the other players are insulting me. I can't let them just walk over me like that. I'm going to keep fighting as long as they keep insulting me. If you want it to stop, you'll have to let us make it stop."

"Now how would I do that?"

"Well, every time I've gotten in a fight, you've come over and broken it up before we ever get a chance to finish."

"So what's your point?"

"Let us finish. People like resolution, Coach. If you don't let us finish, the anger's still there."

"Joe, I can't allow you guys to fight. I could lose my job for that."

I knew he was right. I didn't want him to lose his job. I rolled over my next words slowly and cautiously, as though each one could be a landmine, "Well, maybe next time a fight breaks out, you could just happen to be looking the other way, chatting with the coaches on the sideline."

Coach thought for a moment. I'll bet the only words going through his mind were, Could I really get away with it? Finally, though, he broke into a nasty grin. "Alright, boy. I'll try your idea. Next time a fight breaks out; I'll turn the other way. But this all stays between you and me. If the word gets out, it's both of our asses."

"Coach," I said, "I don't even know who I would tell if I wanted to."

He gave an uneasy smile as I got up out of my chair. But just before I left the room, he added one last comment, "And Joe . . . if you get your ass kicked in the meantime, don't expect me to pull the other guy off you."

It wasn't long before the next fight broke out. It was the next day, if I remember correctly. Coach was standing on the opposite side of the field and had us running scrimmage plays. Just like the day before, one of the linebackers caught me on the left side and brought me to the ground. It was the same player who had called me a gorilla the day before. As I tried to get up, he threw me back to my knees and said, "Stay down there, nigger! Nobody's coming to your rescue."

He didn't know how right he was. I bent over onto one knee, sucking in large gulps of air, and then I looked over to the sidelines. Coach was standing with his clipboard, surveying all the commotion on field. When he finally met my eyes, I smiled. I'm not sure if he could tell I was smiling, but when I gave a quick nod of my head, it was obvious that he read me loud and clear. He turned to his assistant coach, and I heard him mutter something about a new play he'd just invented. Both of them turned the other way.

My hands were twitching with excitement. I turned to the linebacker. He was already on his way back to the huddle, but I figured I could make us both get a delay of game. I popped up from my knee and leapt onto his back. He let out a large scream as I latched my arm around his neck and wrestled him to the ground. There was no doubt Coach could hear him, but for whatever reason, he seemed preoccupied with something else.

I commenced the beating of a lifetime. The rest of the team huddled around me while I was trading punches between my left and right fists. None of them got involved, probably because they figured someone was on their way over to break us apart, but when nobody came, they didn't know what to do.

With each throw of my fists, a drop of anger seeped its way out of my body. I began to feel invincible. I could see the hatred return to the eyes of my adversary. But there was a point when that hatred turned into fear, and that's when I decided to hold myself back. I used the young man's body as a brace to push myself upward, keeping the back of his shoulders pressed to the ground. When I got to my feet, I looked down on him, and I saw something that changed me. He was no longer a ravenous killing machine. He was utterly helpless. He was defeated. I reached out my hand and pulled him up.

I would love to say that the anger stopped after that day, but it didn't. It kept on going, and going strong. But though the anger didn't stop, the fighting did. I think that in this case, fighting was the only language that they knew. The intention was not to hurt the other guy. It was to prove myself. I figured that if I could fight, I could win their respect. Once I did that, the fighting stopped and my team began to tolerate my presence a lot more.

The Cafeteria

But just because they tolerated me, did not mean they embraced me. I still received the cold shoulder from most of them.

School still was not in session, so there weren't a lot of other people around. The campus was vacant and it was easy to feel lonely as one of the only people there. But at least for the other guys, they had each other.

During training camp, all the football players would eat in a special cafeteria that was reserved for the team. Each day at lunch, I would take my seat at a small table to one side of the room, and as the rest of the team filed in, they would look at me, look at where I was seated, then take a seat at the other side of the room. As more people came, their crowd became bigger and mine stayed the same. Just my lunch tray and I. I mentioned that I was on the outside of a circle. Well, there in the cafeteria, it seemed less like a metaphor and more like a tangible reality; even the coaches would ignore my presence.

They would take their trays and gather at the other end of the room, some not even bothering to acknowledge me. After a few weeks, Coach White had noticed that it was getting out of hand, so one day after practice he decided to call a team meeting.

There in the locker room, I remember, he pulled no punches. "From now on, I don't ever want to see Joe eating alone! You hear me?! I want you to swarm that man when he's eating! God knows you're treating him like dirt—tomorrow I want him to feel like the king of the universe!" He didn't hesitate to point straight at me. He could have just as well strapped a blazing neon sign to my chest that read, "Coach's pet! Haze me!".

I was lucky, though, because my teammates knew what was best for them. They weren't stupid. If Coach wanted you to do something, you could either do it or kiss your butt goodbye. The very next day when I went to take my seat, I already had a small ring of teammates waiting at my table. I stopped in my tracks, then looked around and went to take a different seat. That's when someone yelled, "Profit!"

I turned around. One of the guys had his foot on the seat of a chair. He kicked it out and pointed for me to sit down. I hesitated. There didn't seem to be any way out of it, so I walked over and sat down in the chair. After a few moments, the guy spoke again. "I saw you knock down that linebacker the other day."

"Yeah," I said.

"So . . . what's your secret?"

I looked at him, smiled, and then dug into my meal.

It still wasn't clear skies after that. In fact, most of the students acting nice were only doing so out of fear of a higher power—Coach White. However, I realized that while I was still far from that inner circle, by sharing a meal with my teammates I could break down some barriers. I could learn more about them, and they about me. Best of all, as time went by they got to find out that I really wasn't such a bad guy after all.

This is where I learned a phrase that I've kept in my life to this day: "Never eat alone." I learned from my days in the cafeteria that you can learn so much about life from talking to just about anyone. Even today when I go on business trips all around the country, I'll go into a restaurant and ask a random person if I can eat with them. I simply say, "I don't like to eat alone". Sometimes they'll look at me like I'm a creep, and sometimes they'll flat out say, "No," but usually I've found that other people are looking for the exact same thing. By sharing meals with complete strangers, you can learn a lot about people in general—what they do, who they live with, and where they find meaning in life. It's also a great way to make connections that might last far beyond the duration of a simple meal.

I also believe that eating together is an integral part of developing family bonds. When we share a meal, we can talk about important things going on in our lives, learn more about each other and grow closer. In the cafeteria, with my teammates around me, that's exactly what happened.

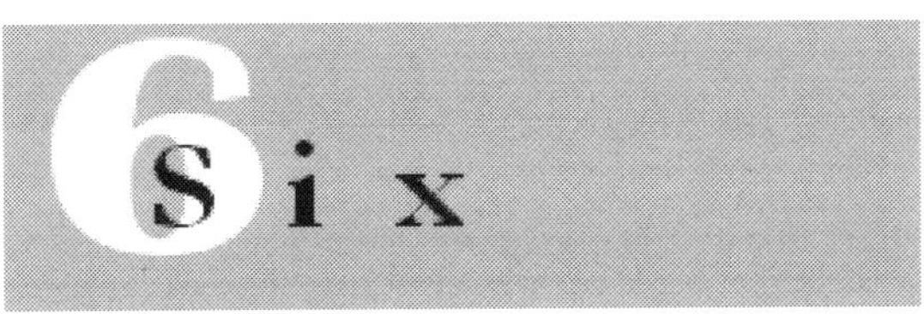

THE WORLD AGAINST ME

The Real Northeast

Once school started, I found it a lot harder to fit in. I wasn't able to hide under the hood of my football team anymore, much less my football coach. There were no rules out on campus. Each time I would walk to class I would be reminded of my "unconformity." People would call me nigger and coon so often I thought for sure they would run out of inventory. Sometimes I would bump into someone and they would call me both. If I was really lucky, they would get their friends to join in on the chiding. At those times, I would feel more than just pain. I would feel lonely. The worst part was that they all had their friends to lean back on for support. If one couldn't take me down, there would surely be another one nearby to finish the job. But me, I was all alone.

Sometimes the comments weren't even mean spirited, but they would still get under my skin simply because they reminded me that I was constantly noticed. Somebody would whisper to their friend, "There's that black kid. Yeah, it's really him. I heard about him." Moreover, I would be forced to walk across campus knowing that I was being watched. I was constantly self-conscious, and it was tiring and emotionally deteriorating.

Nevertheless, there were two places on campus where I felt

refuge. The first was at The Wesley Foundation. The Wesley Foundation was a place of inter-faith camaraderie, where it didn't matter if you were a Protestant, Catholic, Jew, Muslim, Hindu, black, white, brown or whatever. You were welcome as you were. You were respected as you were. For me, that was the best part.

At the Wesley Foundation, I was able to share my story of faith, and my story of adversity. The people there were genuinely interested, too. I think it intrigued them to see how different I was, and they were eager to hear my story—and I was definitely an intriguing storyteller. It was a great place to shed a light of acceptance on my university. Just like on the football team, once the people got to know me, they began to understand and respect me.

The other place I felt comfortable was the Young Republicans Club. The students there showed me that the political world did not have to be filled with so much hatred, and I think that's what appealed to me the most. At the club meetings, we would get together and discuss different matters of the world, and both conservatives and liberals were welcome to attend, which made for some good discussions. The point was not to argue, but rather to promote a healthy, constructive and open-minded conversation so that we could better the world. Many times, the topic would turn to race, and I would dominate the discussion. Again, people were able to hear a side of the story with which they were unfamiliar. I was able to open the minds of the students who attended, and that had an exponential effect on the campus. Once they started accepting me, they began sharing my story with their friends. The acceptance began to trickle across the campus.

It was a blessing that I had been able to become involved in the community. It was still early in my collegiate career, but I had already infiltrated the sporting world, the religious world and the political world—at least, on campus. But these were only small portions of the campus population, and even smaller portions of the population at large. It would take a long time before I began to gain the wider respect of my fellow men.

The First Start

"Now, when you boys head out onto that field today, I want you to keep yourself protected! Look out for one another! Make sure you stick together, and for God's sake keep your helmet on your head!" We all knelt down in a circle around Coach White in the tiny locker room at Stephen F. Austin State University. The words bellowed from his mouth, but they were instantly absorbed by the roaring of the stadium crowd above. Normally, this kind of a pep talk would be expected before the game, but this time it was different. Coach White's words had nothing to do with the game plan or football strategy—they were about survival.

I kept my knee firm to the ground, but my head bent over in prayer instead of looking up at the coach. I knew that this game was about much more than a win or a loss. For me, for my team, for my family and my race, this game was a statement. I remembered the words of my dad again, "Things aren't going to get any better if nobody does anything." In the locker room there, I knew I was going to help make things better. But the path ahead was going to be rocky.

I had been shaking the entire day, and it had only gotten worse as the game time approached and the crowd got louder. Coach kept shouting out his orders but I couldn't pay attention. Earlier in the week, he had taken me aside and told me he had been pondering whether to start me in the game or not. It wasn't a question of skill—I knew I was good enough and so did he. The problem was Coach White was legitimately scared for me, and he was scared for his team. Finally, he let me know he'd made a decision, and that I would be starting on special teams.

Coach's speech was drawing to a close. I felt the shoulder pads around me rise up, letting me know that it was time to go. I stayed down for one more second, then threw my helmet over my head, strapped it on and got to my feet. The tunnel to the field scared me. From the other end I could hear the darkening screams of fans, but I couldn't see the things in their hands—the cups, the bottles, all the trash—that would soon be raining down on my head. As my teammates all made their way down that tunnel, Coach White stayed back to talk.

"You alright, son?"

I couldn't nod or shake my head. I couldn't move. It was a totally different environment than I was used to. Before then, I had only played in high school where the crowds were small and the games were safe. I didn't know that it could get like this. Coach put his hand on my shoulder and said, "C'mon, Joe. Just keep your helmet on." I finally turned to him as he was already headed down the tunnel, and I couldn't help thinking he would need a helmet just as much as me.

I took the first step out of the locker room. The noise was already twice as loud. I felt like I was in a surreal dream where there was so much noise, I could not perceive what was happening. Slowly, my feet began to move again. The noise became louder. As I took my first step into daylight, I knew the tunnel had taken me straight into hell.

The other team's mascot was the Lumberjack, and the people in the bleachers surrounded me in a sea of waving souvenir axes. When I came into view, and the fans saw that a black person was stepping onto their field, the axes began slowly changing direction. Their blades glinted in the sunlight, and to me they were no longer souvenirs. They were real axes, and they were pointing straight at me, ready to slice me to pieces. It was the first time I had ever feared for my life.

"Nigger!" Somebody yelled. I felt a cup graze the side of my helmet. Then others joined in. Before I could even join my teammates, the stadium was swarming with a chant of "Nigger! Nigger!" and I felt my heart begin to ache. It felt cold. There's no analogy for it—the whole world was against me. I closed my eyes and tried to block it out. Again I started thinking of the words my dad had told me, but much like Coach's pep talk, the words in my mind flooded out by the barrage of hateful voices around me.

I got to the sideline and tried to find somewhere I could hide from the fans, but there was nothing. Coach came over to me and yelled through my ear hole, "Keep your helmet on, Joe!" He'd said it before, but now I could see what he meant. Our team had won the coin toss at mid field, and Coach was about to send me out for the opening kickoff.

He pushed my shoulder, and I stayed still. He pushed me again. I still didn't move, because I honestly didn't believe it was my time. Coach pushed me again, practically dragging me this time, and I finally started running to the field.

I took my place at the goal line. The stadium was still chanting, "Nigger! Nigger!" and the fans in the seats behind me were beating their axes against their bleachers. It sounded like thunder, trying to scare me, chase me away. My heart was on overdrive, but I couldn't hear it over the noise of the stadium, and I couldn't feel it over the pounding of the axes.

Before I knew it, the whistle was blown and the ball was kicked off the tee. I started tracing its path, trying to anticipate where it was going to land. But as I followed it through the sky, something changed inside me. My eyes were no longer focused on the ugliness that ensued in the stadium below. None of that mattered. Right then, my mind was focused on things above. All there was now was a football.

I caught the ball and sunk my foot deep into the paint of the five yard-line. Immediately, I started scanning the field. There were some blockers forming together just to my left, so I cut left and followed behind them. It was incredible, then, because the whole time I had felt like I was being buried under a wall of white people, but now a wall of white people was forming to protect me, to save me. They blasted through a group of Lumberjacks and opened a hole down the side. All I remember seeing then was blue sky and green field. I took the ball 95 yards for the score.

As I ran back to the sideline, Coach White was beckoning me over with his hand. I thought to myself, oh Lord; all hell has broken loose now. I walked over to his side, he pulled me in close. He yelled, "Take your helmet off, son!"

I shook my head no. I knew what I had done, but the crowd

was still chanting, and I wanted all the protection I could get from their hateful words. But then coach took my chinstrap and yanked it off. "Take your helmet off, son! Listen! Listen!"

I pushed up my faceguard and pulled the helmet off my head. It was then that I heard it. "Go Joe Go! Go Joe Go!" The sea of angry fans had turned its tide.

Coach pulled me in close once more. He looked me in the eye, and this time I could hear him loud and clear. He said, "That's how you change attitudes, son. Good work."

We won the game, 7-6.

I learned a great lesson that day about the nature of people, and how such a small thing can impact our perceptions. When we get down to the core of it, all I did was run a kick back for a touchdown. But the implications were far greater. That small act changed an entire stadium of people.

It seems that, in life, everyone starts out performing a balancing act. We stand on top of a tall, skinny fence and look down on both sides, one being good and one being evil, and try to decide which one is best. But since the fence is so capricious, even something as small as a feather can tip us in either direction.

<u>Tipping the Fence at Home</u>

That day on the road was one of my most important accomplishments. I was able to get more people on my side, which was by far the most comforting thing to me since I started going to Northeast. What's ironic, though, is that I still wasn't allowed to start a game at home because so many of my own peers were still against me.

During the home games, Coach White would keep me on the sidelines until a few plays had been run with our other running backs. Then he'd tell me once again to get my helmet on, but by then I didn't need any reminding—I had already learned that rule by heart. He'd say, "Get in the game, Joe," and when I ran onto the field, I would run into a sea of boos. Coach White would keep me in and let me run with the offense, but once we got inside the 20 yard line, he'd take me out again and put the others back in so they could score the touchdown.

I don't know why I put up with that for so long. I think it was just because I wasn't in a great position to do anything else.

A reporter once asked to run an article on me for the Monroe News Star. I was surprised. I had never seen a black man in the newspaper before—at least for anything positive. I figured, much like the rest of the campus, that the fans might benefit from hearing my words for once, so I jumped at the opportunity. During the interview, the reporter asked why I didn't say something publicly about the way I was routinely treated on the field. I told the reporter that it wasn't in my power to change anyone's opinion. When asked about being taken out of the game in scoring position, I gave the same answer.

"I am the player, and my coach is the coach." I said. "I would love to stay in the game and score the touchdown, but it's not my decision. My job is to be ready and to give my best whenever the coach needs me."

"You act like you're enjoying this treatment," he said.

"Well, there are some things I can change and some things I can't," I said, "I don't enjoy the treatment at all, but I feel like God has anointed me. He has helped me keep my head up."

Each time I stepped onto the field I was treated nearly the same way as I was at Austin. Nobody in the Northeast crowd—especially the alumni faithful—wanted to see a black boy disgracing their field, and I figured it would take something more than a kick return to tip their fence.

But when the story ran in the news, many people seemed to realize for the first time how unfairly I was being treated. I went to coach's office after practice one day to ask him about it.

"Not only have I seen the story, I've heard a lot from it, too," He said. "Now I get random people in public coming up to me, calling me a racist for not putting you in the game. Like I can do anything about it."

I felt bad about that, but I still didn't see what the problem was, "Why don't you just let me play, then? You've got me who wants me in, you who wants me in, and now a bunch of people who do too." I looked at him with fire in my eyes. I had been doing everything he asked of me. I had practiced hard, gone to class and gotten good grades. None of it made sense.

When he saw the look in my eyes, he motioned to the chair across from him, "Have a seat." I did, and he continued, "Look, son. It's good that people are cheering for you now. God knows we both need more people on our side. But the problem is that there are a whole lot of other people that don't want you in."

He wiped his forehead and let out a sigh, and then he went on, "Let me explain something to you. I understand that it's a very difficult thing, doing what you're doing, but I have difficulties too. Before you came to this team, my wife and I were invited to bridge parties, the

Mayor's Ball and just about every big event this city has to offer. Now, we don't get those invitations. For everyone out there that tells me I'm a racist, I got ten more calling me at night, telling me I'm a nigger lover." His voice was turning hard; his face turning hot. "They've threatened to run me out of town! All for this. All because of you!"

At that moment, I couldn't tell whether Coach loved me or hated me. It sure felt like he was pinning it all on me. Finally, though, his voice began to soften. He leaned over his desk and met my gaze, and it seemed like the tiny office was the only world that existed, and the only people were me and him. He said, "Son, I want you to listen to me. Nobody's going to change their mind. They're too damn stupid. So that's why we're going to have to change it for them."

"But Coach, I've tried. I've played well. What more do I have to do?"

"There's nothing you can do aside from being persistent. People are starting to come around already. You saw it yourself. Just like the game at Austin, the only way we're going to change people's minds is by winning. Now, I'll try to get you into the games when I can, but I can't sacrifice the safety of our players and staff in the process.

"Okay," I said."

"Boy, mark my word. If you keep playing hard, one day they'll come around."

More Challenges

I was tested constantly. The world did not quit. I had my willpower tested on the football field, where I worked myself twicc as hard and didn't get to start a game. I had my character tested every day when someone would pass and point out "the nigger kid" to their friends while walking to class. Each day when I would take my seat in class, the others would purposely take the seats farthest away. If they couldn't find a seat far enough away, they would slide their desk as far as they could in that direction. It felt like a re-run of my freshman year training camp in the cafeteria, only this time, Coach White wasn't there to kick them all into shape.

Among those emotional tests, I was tested in the classroom, but not in a way that I had anticipated. Remember that of the three goals I had laid out for myself at the beginning of college, the first was to graduate in four years and make the Dean's List. This came above all, and it was the first and foremost thing expected of me by my parents. But one major roadblock came, and it came in the form of my English professor, Dr. Garrett.

English was never my favorite subject to begin with. I always felt uncomfortable writing essays, and I was very self-conscious about my work. Even worse, I felt bad about underachieving, which made it harder to get back on track and do well.

All those feelings were magnified tenfold when I entered this class. About a week into the semester, I realized that the professor was not too fond of me. He ignored me when I had any questions or comments, and never let me participate in class discussions. It was frustrating, because I couldn't even go to the administration office to complain. Even if they did hear me out, there was no way they would believe a black student over a white professor with a Ph.D. Eventually, I decided my only way to compensate for his negligence was to study extra hard. I figured once the class was over, I would be able to file it away in the back of my mind.

We took our first test a few weeks into the semester. I had studied hard all week leading up, but I was still a little bit uncomfortable with the material as I took the test. A few days later, Dr. Garrett posted the grades on the front wall of the classroom. After he dismissed us, the whole class started cramming around the sheet of paper trying to find their grade. Even though I was a running back, I didn't push through the crowd. I figured if I bumped the wrong person, I'd get an earful of hateful words, and frankly I was tired of it constantly happening. So I stayed back. Once everyone left, I stepped up to the sheet and found my name. Profit: 89, D-. I traced over the words again. I ran my finger across the sheet to make sure I hadn't read it wrong, but it was printed in bold ink. Profit: 89, D-. Then I traced my fingers further down the list. Just below my name, there was another student whose grade read: 85, B. Several others had the same score as mine, but theirs all read B+, and nobody seemed to share my grade. The professor was still gathering his papers at the front of the class when I read my grade, so I picked the sheet off the wall and took it over to his desk.

"Dr. Garrett?"

"Is there a problem?" He asked.

"Well, sir." I had a hard time looking at him directly. From my seat at the back of the room it was always difficult to get a good view of him, but up here close and personal I could see all the details for the first time. It was overwhelming. Oddly enough, he looked familiar, but I couldn't figure out why.

With the sheet in my hand, I averted my eyes. I just stared

down and pointed at my name. "Sir, the sheet here says that I got an 89."

He took the sheet from my hand and studied it for a second. "You sure did."

"Yes, but the sheet also says that I got a D-." I kept referring to "the sheet" as if it were the thing that had given me the bad grade. I didn't dare suggest that he had.

He studied the sheet further and repeated, "You sure did." After a moment's pause, in which he didn't even think to question his own integrity, he said, "Any more questions now, Boy?"

He called me boy even though he called everyone else Mr. or Ms. I was okay with being called boy by my parents and my coaches, but here in the classroom we were supposed to be professional. Here, I wasn't a boy. At that, I finally looked to his eyes, and I realized why he looked so familiar. Behind the rims of his glasses were the same repellent eyes of so many students and faculty I had met on campus; the ones who whispered and pointed, the ones who just didn't feel I belonged. I knew then that I had an uphill battle ahead of me. Carefully and kindly, I explained that some of the other students scored lower but had a higher grade.

"I didn't make a mistake," he said. He took the grading sheet and set it down on his desk, out of my sight. Then he turned back to me and said, "Boy, I want you to understand something. No matter what you score in my class, you will never get more than a D-. Is that clear?"

With that my blood started to boil. I wanted to push him into the wall and knock him out cold. He was a dwarf compared to my big running back body. But something held me back. I remembered stories my dad used to tell me of when he was a young man. He told me how, coming back from fighting in the war, he couldn't even go into a restaurant and order a meal because of the color of his skin. Being born as a black kid in one of the poorest places in Louisiana, he'd tell me, I was going to have to run faster, study harder, work longer, work smarter, and keep focused longer than anyone else. His words flashed through my memory then as I stared the professor in the eyes.

So I did nothing. I walked out of the room and out of the building. I walked back across campus to my dorm room in the rain, and I was glad it was raining, because I could pull my hood up and nobody could see me crying. When I got back to my dorm, I slammed the door closed with force. The sound rattled through the rest of the hall. I didn't care. I flung myself onto my mattress and buried my head in my pillow. It was soaked through in minutes.

Time for Me to Quit?

There was nobody else there in my room, because nobody at that school wanted to be roommates with the black kid. I had thought that the hatred would subside with time, but this proved to be false. Most of the people on campus didn't know me, which meant they didn't have any problem hating me. They were long, sharp arrows and I was just a big black target.

I started thinking about the last year and what I had hoped to do and what I had actually done. I didn't have any real friends. I hadn't changed anyone's mind. There wasn't a whole lot I had to show other than some stats on the football field, and even then, I only made the people happy until the beginning of the next game.

I thought about that morning in my kitchen when I decided to go to Northeast. I was trying to convince my dad that I knew what I was doing, but maybe I was trying to convince myself all the same. Now the question ate at my thoughts: Did I really know what I was doing? The answer was no. I didn't sign up for this kind of treatment, and I wouldn't be able to tolerate it until the school started changing. But in my eyes, the school wasn't going to change, and if the school wasn't going to change, there was no point in being there.

I stood up from my bed. I started collecting my things. I threw my footlocker open and propped it up on my mattress, the same way I had at Alcorn. There wasn't a second thought in me. All I cared about was shoveling as much clothing into my arms as possible so I could get myself out of there.

A few minutes later, Bob Grosclose, my track coach, opened my door. He saw the clothes in my hand and the suitcase on my bed.

"What do you think you're doing?" He said.

"Why are you here?" I asked. My voice was angry.

"I saw you walking across campus," he said, "and you looked upset."

"Well, I am upset. That's why I'm packing up and leaving," I said. He didn't respond. He just traced my steps back and forth across the room as I was gathering my clothes and putting them in my footlocker. "I'm sorry, Coach. I've had enough. I just can't take it anymore."

Coach looked devastated. I could see it in his eyes, like I had done something to hurt him. In a way, I felt like I had. Coach

Grosclose was one of the best people I knew at Northeast, and he had helped me build strength and confidence when I was first enduring the hatred. I didn't want to look at him, because each glance at his eyes would remind me of the only thread that still tied me to this school. I didn't want to look at that thread. I wanted to get out of there and forget everything that had happened.

Suddenly, as I dug my hand into my dresser drawer, I saw Coach's hand appear right beside mine. But instead of holding me back, he reached into the drawer and pulled out a handful of shirts.

"Now what do you think you're doing?" I said.

He carried the shirts over to my suitcase and stacked them neatly in the back corner. "What does it look like? I'm helping you pack!"

I looked at him, puzzled. "Why? You want me out of here, now?"

"Hell, Joe, I only want fighters on my team. I thought you were a fighter, but you're just a damn coward."

I squeezed the pair of jeans I held in my hand. Now I was the one staring, and he was the one going back and forth between the dresser and the suitcase. That went on for a few minutes, me just watching him, and the whole time I was infuriated when I should've been happy that this last thread was helping me leave. Finally, when he saw that I wasn't doing anything, he paused. There was a pair of socks in his hand, and he pointed them to my chest like a dagger. "Let me tell you one thing before you leave, though. If you quit now, you will be quitting all your life. As soon as you get a little adversity, you're going to get scared just like you are now and run like a damn chicken."

And that was all it took. I threw the pair of jeans, and they narrowly missed my coach's ear before smacking into the wall behind him. I yelled, "Everyone's too mean, Coach! I can't stand it anymore! I go to bed at night, and when I wake up I pray that I'm somewhere else before I look around and see these walls! This whole place is like a prison to me!" My voice echoed through the open door. I was crying now, but by that time I didn't care if the whole world knew how I felt. If they knew I was angry, sad or scared, it would just give them more reason to hate me, more reason for me to leave.

Coach Grosclose didn't seem to care about any of that, though. He waited for me to finish, then he said really quietly, "Boy, in this life you're going to meet a lot of mean people. They'll beat you down with the way they speak and with the way they behave. But if you quit now, you won't have done a damn thing. If you quit now, they'll strut all over you and say, 'See? I told you he'd quit! I told you he was weak!'"

I just looked down at the floor, and he continued speaking, "Joe, look at what you're doing here," He spread out his hands, indicating not just "here" in the dorm room, but "here" in the entire world. "Look at it all. It's not just about you anymore. What you're doing now is about a whole race of people who are depending on you. They're depending on you to stay the course and do the right thing, but now you're just going to throw it in their face?"

I thought back to my dad and how I said I was doing the right thing. I thought back to how I threw the scholarship at Alcorn in his face. That's when I realized that coach was right. I was going to keep running from my problems my whole life. I didn't want to do that.

I turned my head away from the floor. Now I saw my coach's

eyes again. I saw the thread that tied me to the university, and I realized it was stronger than I thought. "Coach," I said, "I don't want to disappoint anyone."

"Well that's what you're doing, Boy."

"I know." I walked over to him. He looked like he was on the verge of tears now. That's when I realized how much I truly meant to him. I was an impact in his life. If I had done that much, then maybe there was still more I could do. I reached for his hand, grabbed the pair of socks then threw them back in my drawer.

"That's my boy." He said. We both started crying, and I took him into my arms. We stood there and hugged for a long time. Once again, I didn't care if anyone saw me or heard me, but this time it was because I was proud.

I went back to class with a new energy that I hadn't felt in a long time. For the second test in Dr. Garrett's class, I prepared even harder than I had for the first one. I went back home to Richwood and asked some of my old English teachers to help me study. When the time for the test came, I felt more prepared than any of the other students. When Dr. Garrett posted the grades once again, I saw that I scored a 95, but I was only given a C-. But I stood my ground and didn't say a word.

I remember when Coach Freeze gave us that pep talk after the Richwood football team's first loss. He told us to turn our roadblocks into stepping stones. That's how I decided to treat the obstacles I faced at Northeast. When Dr. Garrett made my grade lower than it should have been, it made me work harder. There's no other way I would have worked so hard at an English class, and there's no other way I would have learned so much. As much as I'm sure he would have liked to differ, Dr. Garrett's negligence did me a favor in the end.

I would love to say Dr. Garrett came around, but he never came around and I never got higher than a C-. Regardless, I completed the course; I put it in the past, and I kept moving forward. Today, I am proud that I had the character to stand down from Dr. Garrett, instead of hitting him like I wanted to. I was still angry at him for long after that class was over, but it eventually faded.

I'm not mad or bitter about the way I was treated at Northeast. At the time, it nearly beat me to the ground, but now when I look back, I realize that it made me a stronger person. It taught me to persevere. My dad had told me that as a black man, I would have to work twice as hard. He said if the teacher asked for an hour of study, I'd have to do two. If the trainer demanded fifty pushups, I'd better get ready for 100. But all that extra work only made me better in the end. Nowadays, the hard work is embedded in my DNA. It has made me stronger and more determined so that I know I can do anything—and do it twice as well.

The best lesson I can give is that adversity is tough. We face it not just in the color of our skins but in every regard. As easy as it is to write these words, it's a whole different game when putting it into action. People like my professor will hit hard, and you'll want to hit back, but if you do, you'll be lowering yourself to a whole different standard—one that you're not meant for. As hard as it is to hear, your best option is to keep strong and keep improving, even when you're sure you'll never win in the short run.

Seeing the Benefits of Adversity

After I received the bad grade in Dr. Garrett's class, I was down on myself for quite some time. I didn't want to show my grades to my parents, because I knew they would take no excuses for the "bad" performance. Thus, I kept myself busy on campus so that I wouldn't have to keep my mind preoccupied. I was performing well on the track team with the help of Coach Grosclose, a living legend at Northeast. He was similar to Coach White, in that he didn't care whether I was black or white as long as I could perform. With his coaching, I was able to drop my 100-yard dash time down to 9.5 seconds.

My teammates on the track team were welcoming to me as well. As soon as they saw how fast I was, they didn't have much of a reason to treat me unfairly. I met and became good friends with two runners in particular, John Hollingsworth and Don Warren, both from Jackson, Mississippi. Those two gave me a reason beyond the sport itself to look forward to going to practice, and that meant a lot to me.

I also kept myself busy with the Young Republicans. It felt good to have somewhere to go where I could vent my frustrations. When I revealed the story about Dr. Garrett, many of my peers encouraged me to try to take action against him, but I felt that it was a futile and pointless pursuit. I was done with it and didn't care to make any more of a deal of it. I just enjoyed having people around who would listen to me speak. That was a rarity on that campus.

Those two outlets provided an amazing feeling of hospitality for me. They gave me friendships in a time of desperate need. But they still didn't provide that same sense of companionship of my friends from home, simply because they didn't share my roots. It was difficult for them to relate to me, and me to them. For this reason, as friendly as they were, it was hard to connect fully with them.

There were almost no black people on campus at that time, and what I noticed more specifically was that I had never seen a black girl on campus. This was hard for me, because I was in desperate need of that full companionship, but there was a large stigma against inter-racial relationships that I couldn't afford to test.

Fortunately, one day I did meet a black girl on campus. Her name was Deborah. I couldn't figure out why I hadn't seen her before—usually folks like us would try to find each other so we could stick together, and it wasn't hard to find each other, since we stuck out from the crowd anywhere we went. I began talking to her, and found out that she was still a senior in high school, but was working an internship on campus.

She returned every few days to keep working, and each time she did, I just happened to pass by.

"Deborah!" I would say, "It's good to see you again." It wasn't long at all before both of us could see through my façade. I was a bit obvious, I admit, but I couldn't help myself. I was young, big, strong and confident. I asked her on a date one day, and flashed her one of the best smiles I could muster. Of course, she accepted. How could she refuse?

We began dating soon after that, and before I knew it, I was in love. We spent as much time together as we could in between school, track practice and the internship. Eventually I ran out of excuses to stop by her work every day, but I still went regardless. She even began making excuses to come to campus 'for work' as often as she could. It was a beautiful time—perhaps the first time that I had ever felt truly comfortable while away from home. I knew that it was special.

Feeling the Pressure From All Sides

But of course, Deborah and I couldn't be together all the time. She had obligations to her school and to her family. I understood that she had to put in her time elsewhere because she had a life outside of mine.

On those days that she wasn't there, I felt the familiar loneliness seep back into the walls of my dorm room and follow me around campus.

Being away from home—even though it was only on the other side of town—changed the way I saw the world. It changed me inside. I was no longer naïve to what the word racism actually meant. I was a veteran of the word. People hated me for doing nothing wrong, but I had no way to convince them to think otherwise. At night, I would lie in my bed and wonder if the Klan would be coming for me. It was a recurring nightmare that would start over each morning.

Living away from home also meant that I lost a part of myself. Most importantly, I was no longer with the people who loved me. They were cut from my life, and a hollow feeling had moved in.

When I returned home, expecting and even hoping for the safe haven of my neighborhood, I found that things were drastically different than I had expected. What I didn't realize was that the people back home—my friends, the community, and just about everybody outside of my family—saw me in the same way as they saw everyone on the Northeast campus. Where a white student would call me a 'nigger,' my friends from high school would accuse me of sucking up to the white people, and call me a 'white lover' or a 'sellout.'

We had always grown up talking smack about the white people on the other side of town, but it was simply because we didn't know much about them. It hurt me to know that the same people had I done that with now felt the same about me. I soon realized that the same isolated feeling from school had followed me home, and the oasis that I was expecting was a terrible lie. I began to learn that hatred does not come in color.

Amid all this hatred that bore down on me from all sides, I went to the only place of refuge I knew would be there: the tiny, ramshackle house where my family still lived. It seemed strange to me. All my life I had been told that I needed to go to school and get a good job so that I wouldn't end up in a house like that. Now, to me, that house seemed like a castle. I would have done anything to stay there under that roof.

Each time I returned home, I gave my family the same sob story. I was being bullied, and it wasn't fair. But one day, my dad had had enough. He caught me lying in my bed, sinking in my own self-pity, and said, "Son, I can imagine how tough it is, but it won't get any easier if you don't stay the course. I don't know where you'll find your strength, but you've gotta find it somewhere."

"Dad," I said, "that's why I came home. This is where I find my strength."

"Boy, look at you! You found nothing but the sheets on your bed!" My dad had a reason to yell if there ever was one. I just didn't realize it at the time. Here I was bickering about the difficulties of college when he himself had only been allowed to finish the third grade. He said third grade was as high as a black man could go during his time—and that I was lucky to live in such great circumstances. He said, "Joe, I want you to have a better life than I did. I want you to do better than me. But so far, you're not doing a very good job of it."

I got out of bed and sat myself up straight. I even puffed up my chest, trying to look like a strong man to show him better, but nothing could fool my dad. I put myself at ease.

"Joe, you made the decision to go to that school, not me. You said you could handle it. I let you make that decision on your own because you're an adult. But this," he motioned to the mess I'd made with all my stuff lying around the bed, "this isn't adult. Now, we expect you to stay at Northeast, and we expect you to graduate." Before leaving the room, he leaned back in and said, "Son, we'll always be here for you. You know that. But you've gotta find your strength somewhere else if you're gonna survive out there."

I remember again how dad would always urge me to use my mind. In high school, I was a dominant force on the football field, but I could have done better in the classroom. Dad would say, "Joe, I know you can play football. But I want you to show me that you can think." That was how he always started those pep talks about me going to college, and I can still remember the sincerity in his eyes when he said it to me. That's the first reason I ever wanted to go to college—the same reason why I was so eager to pick a hundred pounds of cotton when I was a young boy. I wanted to please my mom and dad. I had seen and heard how they lived, and I had seen how I lived. Neither life was pretty, but my life was better than theirs, so I knew I could make it even better if I used my mind.

That's how I began to find my strength. It was in me, in my family, and in my faith in the Lord. I know that it was through His strength that I began to become more comfortable at Northeast.

The first step, I realized, was to change my attitude. I learned to accept the fact that Northeast was a mean environment. I could bicker all I wanted, but in the end it wouldn't change anything. Quitting, I knew, wouldn't change anything either. It would only be passing the baton to someone braver than me. I didn't want it to happen that way, so I figured the smartest option was to stay the course.

The next step was to humble myself—and that was hard. It meant taking a few steps backward and realizing that I had abandoned the very roots of my upbringing—the power of expectations. I realized that my dad had already provided me with the first part—he had told me his expectations, but I was forgetting the second part, the part about me generating my own expectations.

When I got back to my dorm room that Sunday night, I sat down at my desk with a sheet of paper. I began to remember the three things I had set out to do: one was to graduate in four years and make the Dean's List. Two was to play football in the fall, and three was to run track in the spring.

I took my pen and scratched these three things onto my paper so they were right in front of my eyes (*This is one of the most important pieces of advice I can give you. If you physically record your goals, they'll become more of a reality*). Instantly, these goals of mine seemed more tangible, more conquerable.

When I looked them over, though, I noticed something else that I hadn't seen before. Nowhere on this list did I write anything about race. The word didn't exist. Almost instantly, a weight was lifted off my shoulders. I realized that the whole weight of my race didn't have to rest on my shoulders. It wasn't my intention, and it wasn't my job. I decided then that I would focus more strongly on my three original goals. I knew that if I focused on them, helping my race would come as a byproduct, because doing the right thing—and doing it the right way—always has a positive impact.

CHANGING THEIR MINDS

Junior Year

The next summer, I received some of the best news in all my time at Northeast. My best childhood friend, Don Zimmerman, had decided to transfer to Northeast. I couldn't believe it when he told me. I nearly suffocated him when I hugged him.

I said, "Donny, you have no idea what this means to me! All my time on campus I've been waiting to make some black friends, and now I've finally got somebody that I already know."

He was pretty happy, too. He said, "Thanks, Joe, but you know I didn't do this for you. I just needed a place closer to home, was all."

But that didn't matter to me. I felt for the first time that I would be able to feel comfortable on campus—where I would have someone who understood me and where I came from. A few weeks later, as school was fast approaching and both of us were on campus for a visit, I finally said, "So Don, what are you going to try out for this fall? You going to play quarterback?"

But Don just shook his head. He said, "Joe, I haven't told you this—I haven't told anyone this, except my family—but I'm not planning on playing football here."

My eyes went wide. In all my life, I had never seen Don more than ten feet away from a football. I couldn't imagine him any other way—and I certainly couldn't imagine him transferring to a white school just because the academics were good. It just didn't make sense.

"What do you mean, you're not planning to play football?"

"Exactly what I said. I got an opportunity to get a college degree. I'm not going to waste my time on the football field. That would only be a distraction."

"A distraction? I exclaimed, "What is that bullshit?" I grabbed his arm and threw him over my shoulder."

He screamed and struggled in my arms, "Hey! What're you doing?!"

"Donny, I'd love to hear you out, but you're talking crazy right now. Come on, we're going to go see a friend of mine."

I took him to Coach White's office. Coach was on campus preparing for training camp, and he was surprised to see me when I came through his door. He was more surprised to see another black kid struggling beside me.

"Joe, my boy, what are you doing here?"

Finally, I let go of Don and set him down on the floor. "Coach White," I said, "this here is my best friend Don Zimmerman. But more importantly, he's your new quarterback."

We all sat down and talked about the football program, even though Don may have been a little reluctant. But throughout the conversation, it became clear to Don that Coach White treated people with respect. When we left his office, Don said to me, "Joe, I'll be honest with you. I didn't expect that kind of treatment. If everyone else on the team is the same way, I just might try out for the team after all."

Well, I knew perfectly well that plenty of people were not the same way, but I decided to leave that part out for the time being. A few weeks later, Don joined me on the field for the first day of training camp as a walk-on. I was so proud of him, and I was proud of myself for helping him make the decision. Three years later, he would be drafted as a wide receiver by the Philadelphia Eagles. To this day, I still joke with him that I was the only reason he made it in football.

My junior year of college would prove to be the turning point of my tenure at Northeast. During the previous two football seasons, I had played most of the games, but I had never started, and I was rarely allowed to score. Despite these drawbacks, I had still set a school record for rushing yards in a season during my sophomore year. Coach, of course, had told me that he wanted to put me in more, but he had some criticisms raining down from all sides for simply letting me play on his roster. But by then, the tables had turned. We weren't winning enough games as a team, and now the criticisms were harder. Finally, it became clear that the fans didn't care—black or white, just win some games! Coach was given the ultimatum, so he had to give me the green light.

I ran onto the field for the first home game, and I was received by a sea of roaring fans. It was hard to believe that they were cheering for me. They were the same students who would spit at me on my way to class, and call me names just loud enough so that they knew I could hear. Well, they were no longer spitting or calling names. Once I donned the uniform, I was their hero. It was a bit hypocritical, I must say, but I didn't let any animosity get in between us. I soaked in all the respect I could get.

In that sea of fans that day were Deborah, my mom and my

dad. They made a point to come to as many games as possible—something they did for all of their children, but I admired them for coming to my games, especially, because I knew how uncomfortable it made them to cross over into the white side of town. The fact that they were dipped into a stadium of thousands of white people didn't make it any easier on them, but they stuck with it.

In the latter part of the season, though, my dad missed his first game. I knew he wouldn't miss it unless he had a really good reason, so I wasn't bothered that he didn't show. After the game, when I asked my mom where he was, she told me, "Baby, he's in the hospital. He's got pneumonia, but he'll be alright." My heart stopped when she told me he was in the hospital, but I trusted her judgment that he was okay. "Working too hard," my mom added, "The man's never taken a sick day in his life. God knows he could use one."

That's always how I remember my dad. In my entire life, he never missed a day of work. He never took a sick day, and he never, ever took a vacation. That wasn't his way. Caring for his family was too important to him.

In spite of his wishes, he was made to stay in the hospital for the whole week. It was unprecedented in our family. The house felt empty when I visited one afternoon, even though there were plenty of people there to fill it up. When we sat around the dinner table that night, there was nothing but silence. We couldn't imagine carrying on a conversation without the beautiful, charming attitude that my dad brought to the table.

When the following weekend came around, he was practically jumping out of his bed to get home. The doctors said that they would be able to release him on Saturday night, which meant that he would have to miss another one of my games, which was Saturday evening. When I visited him that morning before leaving on the team bus, he was sitting up talking with me. He had a bright smile on his face, even though I could tell he was disappointed that he couldn't go with me.

"Joe, don't you worry about me," he said when I tried to comfort him, "Right now I'm so proud of you I could burst. You go play the best game of your life. You know I'll be with you, even if I'm not really with you."

The Biggest Loss of My Life

I boarded the bus with high hopes. We were headed to Hammond, Louisiana to play Southeastern Louisiana University. It was a game that we were expected to win by a large margin, though I would soon be reminded in a very different way that expectations are not always a guarantee.

It was halftime. I was already well on my way to a 100-yard game, and I didn't see anything slowing me down in the second half. Coach White gave us a short pep talk in the locker room and told us to stay the course. If we kept playing, and I kept running, we would easily walk away with our heads held high. We ran back out onto the field for second half warm-ups, and that's when I heard the news. They announced it out loud over the intercom. My dad had died. To this day, I do not know why they could have been so cruel as to let me find out in that way, in front of the whole stadium, in front of my teammates and my friends. All I could do was drop to my knees, and bury my head in my hands.

There was no sense of time at all. I was alone in darkness and in silence. It felt like hours before anyone came to my side. I finally felt a hand on my shoulder, and heard the voice of Coach White. I was so distraught that I couldn't make out what he said, but that didn't matter because I refused to speak. I felt him grab my shoulder and pull me upward, and I followed him like a thoughtless sleepwalker. He led me over to the sideline, and my teammates parted to give me a path to the bench.

"Sit down, Son." He helped me down to the bench, but I fell limp and quickly went back to my knees. With my body bent over on the grass, I felt the urge to vomit. None of my teammates spoke to me—and I didn't blame them.

There was still time before the second half began, so Coach stuck with me for a minute. "Joe, you need to leave, you just get up and leave," he said, "God knows family is more important than a game."

I still did not speak. I wouldn't have been able to if I tried. All I could think about was my dad's face while he was looking back at me that morning, sitting in his hospital bed with a bright, radiant smile. How could that have been the face of a dying man?

For the first time, I looked up from the ground. I saw the faces of Coach White, Don Zimmerman and a several other teammates. They were all crowded around me, bearing down with their looks of concern. I couldn't take it. I was so overwhelmed that I did the only thing in the world that still made any sense to me. I grabbed my helmet, strapped it on and ran out onto the field.

"Joe!" I heard Don call after me, "Get off the field! You need to go home!" If anyone knew me best on that field, it was Don. He was heartbroken too. He knew just how much my dad had meant to me.

But I kept running. As soon as I got out to the middle of the field, I felt a presence wash over me. I knew the Lord was speaking to me. The lights of the stadium flooded into my eyes, and I could see nothing from the outside world. The fans were gone. The players were gone. The football field was gone. All that was left was me and my mind. I had to keep playing. It's what my dad would have wanted. In all my years, he had never taken a day off from work. Why would I?

I told Coach White that there was no way I was going home. He didn't know what to do, so he shrugged his shoulders and put me in the game.

By the grace of God alone, I was able to finish the game that night. In the second half, I was an unstoppable force. I pulled no punches. I ran like the wind and I didn't look back. When the final whistle blew, I had gained more yards and scored more touchdowns than any other game in my life.

Some people said I was delirious to want to keep on playing in that game. They said I was in shell shock. But I knew differently. I knew it was what my daddy would have wanted. When I left him earlier that day, he had been smiling, he was happy, and most importantly, he was so proud of his boy. That's what I'll remember. He was so proud that I had gotten to where I was. He was proud that I had made the team, that I had stuck with my values and stayed in school, and that I was on my way to earning a college degree. He was so proud.

Learning to Move on: The Power of Prayer

In the months before his passing, my dad received a promotion at his job. It was the first time in his life that things were starting to look up. In all my years, when I said my prayers each night, the only prayer that ever remained constant was for my dad to live long enough for me to provide for him financially. I wanted him to have the chance to retire. I wanted him to see his grandkids. I wanted him to see the value that blossomed from his endless labor.

I have always believed in the power of prayer. It was a part of my upbringing. My mother always said, "Be strong in your work, but don't forget to be strong in your prayers too. Let God do his work. He can use your work, but you're a fool if you think he needs it to do his."

To my dismay, my dad never got to see any of those things that I wanted him to see, but I take comfort in knowing that he saw them on the horizon. He could see that better days were ahead for all of us, and I know that that made him happy.

It was hard for me after my dad passed away. I struggled and wrestled with it for years and years. But by the grace of God, I was finally able to move on. The Lord opened my eyes and showed me all of the wonderful blessings that my dad had given me. He showed me that my dad had left behind a legacy that I was meant to continue. I realized that my dad was and always would be with me in my heart, as long as I remembered the things he taught me. Eventually, I learned to stop thinking of my dad's life as a shortened tragedy, and to start thinking of it as a wonderful, gorgeous blessing.

Football Field

Courtesy of ULM Sports Information

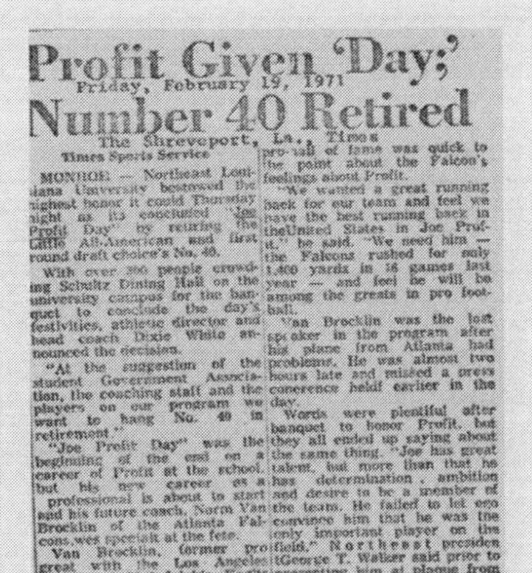

Profit Given 'Day;' Number 40 Retired

Friday, February 19, 1971

The Shreveport, La., Times

Times Sports Service

MONROE — Northeast Louisiana University bestowed the highest honor it could Thursday night as its concluded "Joe Profit Day" by retiring the Little All-American and first round draft choice's No. 40.

With over 300 people crowding Schultz Dining Hall on the university campus for the banquet to conclude the day's festivities, athletic director and head coach Dixie White announced the decision.

"At the suggestion of the student Government Association, the coaching staff and the players on our program we want to hang No. 40 in retirement."

"Joe Profit Day" was the beginning of the end on a career of Profit at the school, but his new career as a professional is about to start and his future coach, Norm Van Brocklin of the Atlanta Falcons, was speciait at the fete.

Van Brocklin, former pro great with the Los Angeles Rams and Philadelphia Eagles ... pro hall of fame was quick to the point about the Falcon's feelings about Profit.

"We wanted a great running back for our team and feel we have the best running back in the United States in Joe Profit," he said. "We need him — the Falcons rushed for only 1,400 yards in 14 games last year — and feel he will be among the greats in pro football.

Van Brocklin was the last speaker in the program after his plane from Atlanta had problems. He was almost two hours late and missed a press conference held earlier in the day.

Words were plentiful after banquet to honor Profit, but they all ended up saying about the same thing. "Joe has great talent, but more than that he has determination, ambition and desire to be a member of the team. He failed to let ego convince him that he was the only important player on the field," Northeast president George T. Walker said prior to presenting him at plaque from the school's administration.

Courtesy of ULM Sports Information

Courtesy of ULM Sports Information

Gale Sayers: "My Football Mentor"

Courtesy of Gale Sayers

Gale Sayers and Joe Profit join in the fight against Sickle Cell Anemia

Courtesy of Dr. Joseph Profit

Football Field

Joe Profit, Halfback, Freshman, Monroe. The first Negro to wear a Northeast athletic uniform; Three touchdowns; 172 yards rushing for a 4.9 average; Had longest run of year for Tribe; 5 pass receptions; Made spectacular TD run against Stephen F. Austin; Fastest man on squad with 9.7 speed.

courtesy of ULM Sports Information

Texas at Arlington: A Tough Opener

Northeast opened its football season by facing one of the nation's highest rated teams in small college football, the University of Texas at Arlington.

Tribe halfback Joe Profit established himself as one of the biggest threats in Gulf States Conference play in the 24-14 opening loss. Profit handled the ball four times in the game, picking up 82 yards, including a 71-yard touchdown jaunt for the first score of the season for the Tribesmen.

Al Miller, all-conference end, hauled in a Steve Mansur pass for the other Indian tally.

Courtesy of ULM Sports Information

Joe Profit runs for a TD!

Courtesy of ULM Sports Information

Northeast Louisiana University 1967 Football Team: Joe Profit, #40, the First Black to Integrate the Football Team

courtesy of ULM Sports Information

Football Field

Courtesy of Atlanta Falcons

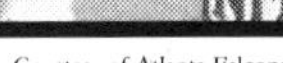

Courtesy of Atlanta Falcons

Courtesy of New Orleans Saints

Courtesy of New Orleans Saints

Courtesy of the WFL

Courtesy of the WFL

Football Field

Profit altered attitudes

Profit's forte involved more than football

Courtesy of Atlanta Journal Constitution

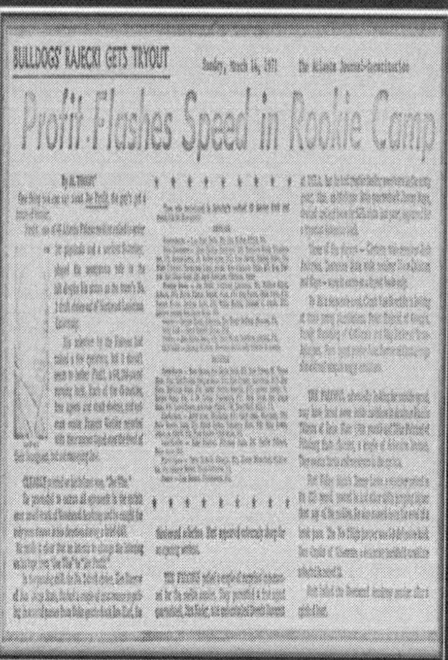

BULLDOGS' RAJECKI GETS TRYOUT

Profit Flashes Speed in Rookie Camp

Courtesy of Atlanta Journal Constitution

Sayers Gone; Profit's Here

By FRANK HYLAND

The Atlanta Journal

SPORTS

Monday, Sept. 11, 1972 1-D

See PROFIT, Page 3-D

Profit Is Falcons' Sayers

Continued from Page 1-D

Courtesy of Atlanta Journal Constitution

ZOOK 'GAINS' ON TOUCHDOWN

Defense, Profit Illuminate Falcon Darkness

Sunday, September 3, 1972 — The Atlanta Journal-Constitution

By FRANK HYLAND

Courtesy of Atlanta Journal Constitution

Tuesday, August 3, 1971 — Atl. Journal-Constitution

FURMAN BISHER

Sports Editor

A Profit With Honor

—A Signing at the Wire

—Circuitous Route to Home

—This Is the Place

See FURMAN BISHER, Page 5-C

Tuesday, August 3, 1971 — The Atlanta Journal 5-C

FURMAN BISHER

Continued from Page 1-C

Courtesy of Atlanta Journal Constitution

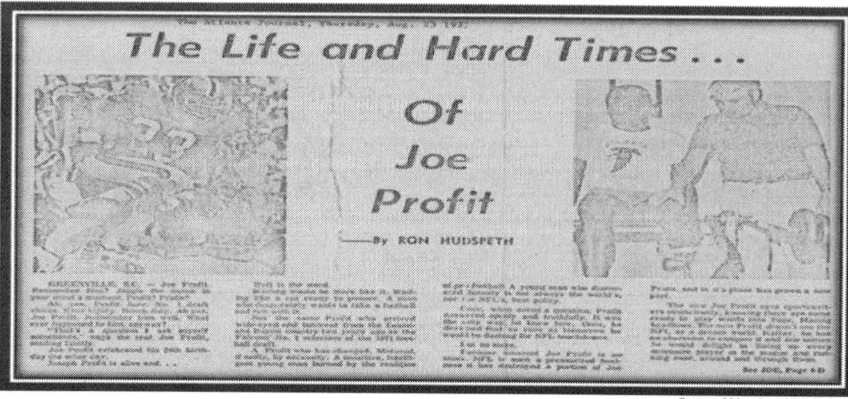

The Life and Hard Times . . .

Of Joe Profit

—By RON HUDSPETH

See JOE, Page 4-D

Courtesy of Atlanta Journal Constitution

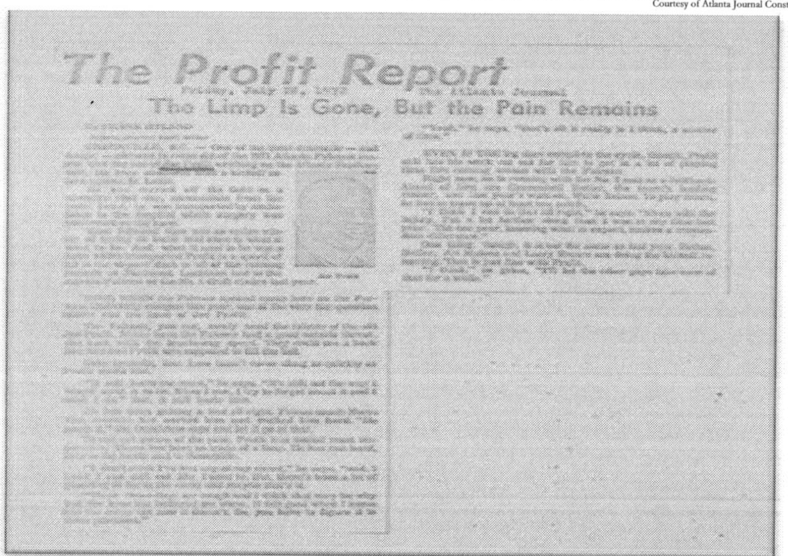

The Profit Report

The Atlanta Journal

The Limp Is Gone, But the Pain Remains

Joe Profit

Courtesy of Atlanta Journal Constitution

Louisiana

Profit to deliver NLU address

Profit

Courtesy of News Star World

The News-Star

SUNDAY, June 27, 1999

Sports

Preps 8

Outdoors 6

Harris, Profit left indelible marks

■ Area sports legends honored with Louisiana Sports Hall induction.

Bryant's Addition athletes still making 'hood proud

T. SCOTT BOATRIGHT

Courtesy of News Star World

James "Shack" Harris (Pro-Bowl MVP) and Joe Profit at Press Conference

Courtesy of Dr. Joe Profit

Coach Dale Brown and Joe Profit paused for a picture at their Induction into the Louisiana Sports Hall of Fame

Courtesy of Dr. Joe Profit

Football Field

ACCENT 1B

Churches full of local history for people, area

SPORTS 1C

NLU football great to join La. Sports Hall of Fame

Joe Profit

The News-Star

SATURDAY, June 26, 1999

Running back Joe Profit played for Northeast from 1967-70.

Profit's bottom line is success

■ Former NLU standout has toiled off field to become top businessman.

La. Sports Hall of Fame

This is the final part of a series of stories on the 1999 Louisiana Sports Hall of Fame induction class.

The inductees, Billy Allgood, Dale Brown, Dave Dixon, James Harris, Rickey Jackson, Joe Profit and Pat Studstill, will be honored today in Natchitoches.

News-Star news services

Before Anthony McFarland, before Kevin Faulk, before Shaun King and Troy Edwards, there was Joe Profit.

There were many outstanding black performers playing college football in Louisiana before 1967 but all of them played for Grambling State or Southern. None played for the state's traditionally white colleges.

The man who broke the state's color barrier in college football and paved the way for modern stars like McFarland, Faulk, King, Edwards and hundreds of black players before them was Profit, a running back and track standout at Northeast Louisiana.

Profit will be one of seven former athletic greats inducted into the Louisiana Sports Hall of Fame today.

"It's a wonderful honor to go into the Hall of Fame with great athletic figures like these and others," said Profit. "I remember when I was a kid hearing about players like Y.A. Tittle, Jimmy Taylor and Billy Cannon and listening to their games on the radio. To be together with them in the State Hall of Fame is a great thrill for me."

Although he is best remembered today in Louisiana for being a racial pioneer, Profit has plenty of other qualifications for fame, both during and after his sports career.

As an athlete, he was an all-American, the all-time leading rusher in the old Gulf States Conference, NLU's career yardage champ until the 1990s, and the seventh player selected in the 1971 National Football League draft.

For some sports stars, the end of their playing career is the end

See PROFIT / 4C

Insid

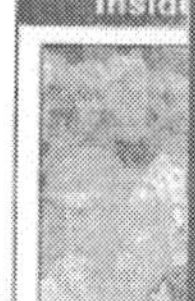

Courier adv

After surviving marathon match blelon, Jan Cour hospitalized for tion.

Story,

Courtesy of News Star World

Running back Joe Profit,
TheNFL League-Leading rusher

Courtesy of Dr. Joseph Profit

Joe Profit Makes the Finalist at the World Body Building Championship Competition

Other Sports

NLU Track - Joe Profit
World Class Sprinter
40 Yard Dash: 4.3 Seconds
100 Yard Dash: 9.5 Seconds

Courtesy of ULM Sports Information

Bob Groseclose (Track Coach) and Joe Profit

Courtesy of Dr. Joseph Profit

World Champion Evander " The Real Deal" Holyfield with Profit at a Golf Outing

Profit Putts for Charity

Courtesy of Dr. Joseph Profit

. . . But Profit's A Millionaire

Profit

Courtesy of Atlanta Journal Constitution

Dr. Joseph Profit boards his private plane to radio TV premier of his show (After the Game with Joe Profit tm)

Courtesy of Dr. Joseph Profit

Dr. Profit prepares to entertain his jet-set clients aboard his newly aquired Private Plane

Courtesy of Dr. Joseph Profit

Communications International, Inc.

NETWORK CONNECTION

COMMUNICATIONS INTERNATIONAL GROWTH, PROFESSIONALISM HONORED AT ENTREPRENEUR BANQUET

CII PRIMARY CONTRACTOR AT KING'S BAY NAVAL SUBMARINE BASE

Courtesy of CII

Profit meets with his Middle East Director of Operations in the United Arab Emirates

Courtesy of Dr. Joseph Profit

The Network Connection

Communications International, Inc.

COMMUNICATIONS INTERNATIONAL SECURES KUWAIT CONTRACT

Courtesy of CII

Don King and Joe Profit discuss upcoming events in Miami

Joe Reeder and Profit assist Hurricane Katrina victims

Mark "Ranger" Jones, Joe R. Reeder, Louis R. Butler and Joe Profit in New Orleans "Katrina Evacuation Team"

About Millionaire Joe Profit

Taken from the Atlanta Constitution

Courtesy of Atlanta Journal Constitution

THE NATION'S NEWSPAPER

SPORTS FINAL

$1M, ALMOST

NO ARBITRATION: McREYNOLDS TO GET $975,000 1C

▶ HEARINGS FOR BELL, GOODEN WEDNESDAY

▶ 2ND SEASON FOR TOP ROOKIES, 1, 7C

GARVEY: Boy Scout image still intact, 2C

AIR JORDAN TAKES OFF; BULLS WIN 1, 8C

WEEKLY NBA STATS, 9C

USA TODAY

NO. 1 IN THE USA . . . 5,541,000 READERS EVERY DAY

TUESDAY, FEBRUARY 16, 1988

NEWSLINE

After the game

Special Report: Page 5B

Some former star athletes find they can score big on a different playing field: business. From restaurants to electronics, the stars play to win by putting lessons from sports — teamwork and coaching — to work.

JOE PROFIT: Ex-football player turned to electronics

PROFIT: Ex-running back's electronics firm is among the USA's fastest-growing businesses.

Profit scores on new grid

Electronics buff runs his company 'like a team'

Joe Profit was intrigued by gadgets while growing up in Monroe, La. But schools there didn't offer electronics courses, so he diverted his energy into football. As it turns out, football was his ticket to high-tech success.

Profit owns Communications International Inc., a Norcross, Ga., firm that installs fiber-optic systems, radar, computer networks and other communications gear. Sales this year may top $15 million, up from $5.7 million in 1986. The company made No. 46 on the 1987 Inc. 500 list of fastest-growing private firms.

The Atlanta Falcons made Profit their top draft pick in 1971, and he played running back in the NFL through 1977. But he didn't wait for his playing days to end to set up his future. In 1974, he bought an International House of Pancakes franchise (the first owned by a black), then sold that and bought several Burger King restaurants. In 1978, Profit started selling surveillance systems — the beginning of Communications International.

After surviving tough early days working out of Profit's basement, "we've been growing every year since 1984," Profit says. The company bought new headquarters in October, and it now employs 300 in 27 states.

Profit's football paycheck helped finance his early ventures, but the sport has helped in other ways. "I try to run the company like I was trained, like a good football team," he says. "We are well-disciplined. We use the word 'coach' a lot, at helping each other. We've made it our lives."

Except for scattered pictures around headquarters of Profit in his playing days, the link with the Falcons doesn't figure into Profit's work. At first, he says, "Football helped open doors." But now, "we've just been working 16-to-20-hour days the last four years."

Courtesy of USA Today

Profit & Success

Communications International, Inc.

By Nancy Creach

Profit 'präfət' n.: advantage or benefit; excess of returns over expenditures; to grow richer; Chairman and CEO of Communications International, Inc.

No matter how you define or describe him, the name Joseph Profit, Sr. means success. As if he were destined to fulfill his name, this mega mogul has climbed the ladder of success in many areas to finally become a powerhouse in the international telecommunications industry. After nearly 14 years, his company Communications International, Inc. (CII) is a corporate force to be reckoned with, and a crown jewel in the Atlanta business community. Headquartered in Norcross, CII operations cover 47 states and three foreign countries, and many CII employees are a virtual who's who of the best and the brightest. Former CII senior vice-president, Catalina Villalpando was appointed United States Treasurer in 1989 by President Bush; Stephen J. Warner, president of Merrill Lynch Venture Capital, Inc., is an active member of the CII board of directors; and Joe Profit himself, was a successful NFL and Atlanta Falcons running back, before becoming the first Black to own an International House of

Joseph S. Profit, Sr.
President and CEO

Pancakes franchise. That marked the beginning of his successful climb to the top of the corporate world.

Communications International, Inc. began as a surveillance systems company in 1979. Now CCI has grown into a sophisticated international telecommunications empire. The company is renowned as a leader in the development, design and installation of an array of intricate telecommunications systems that include international phone systems, military communication units, information technology, and fiber optic networks. CII's ability to capture major contracts with the U.S. Defense Department, the government of Kuwait, Digital Equipment Corp., AT&T, Northern Telecom, and IBM (to name a few), attest to the power of this Atlanta based company. Profit says the success of CII is also due to the mix of a highly skilled and forceful staff, and the vision of its board of directors.

Profit says after 14 years the outlook for CII is great! "We are entering a new dimension of opportunities unlike any that has been experienced by minorities since Lewis H. Latimer, the Black engineer, draftsman and inventor, who worked with Alexander Graham Bell on the process that developed the telephone." Profit says. Bell and Latimer started a revolution, and a 119 year old tradition of discovery and innovation that continues on at CII. Judging by the accomplishments of CII, Profit is clearly synonymous to success.

REINVESTMENT RESOURCE: FIRST UNION NATIONAL BANK

By Nancy Creach

Archibald (Archie) Hill
Manager of Community Reinvestment
First Union National Bank of Georgia

If part of doing good business is giving back to the community, then business is booming at First Union National Bank of Georgia. As Manager of Community Reinvestment, Archie Hill says First Union's commitment to Atlanta's economic development is evidenced in the company's strong statewide programs. The programs are designed to meet the needs of low-to-moderate income communities through established loan pools, the funding of affordable home mortgages, and the development of small and minority owned businesses in Atlanta, and throughout Georgia.

First Union Corporation is the 11th largest bank holding company in the nation. With the power of $53.1 billion in assets behind it, Hill says, "First Union stands ready to assist small businesses either as a provider of financial services, or as a resource contact to point them in the right direction."

Courtesy of CII

GWINNETT BUSI

NEWS TIP? CALL 263-3856

Ex-Falcon Joe Profit Lives Up to His Name With Successful Firm

By Hollis R. Towns
Staff Writer

Twenty years ago, Atlanta Falcons running back Joe Profit traded in cleats for wingtips and his ... old jersey for a snazzy business suit.

After six years of running from defensive linemen in the early '70s, Mr. Profit decided to channel his energy into a new career — running a successful business.

...1984 breakup of American Telephone & Telegraph, when companies such as CI could not compete with Ma Bell — Mr. Profit said he substituted labor for capital, often working into the wee hours of the morning performing secretarial tasks.

"In my first two years, I was bottom-up. We had volunteer help," he said. "But we never gave up. The average person would have given up — saying it's too hard — tired of being given the runaround, having doors closed in your face. We hung in there."

Growing up poor in Monroe, La., had a profound effect on his desire to succeed, Mr. Profit said. He knew his father could not afford to send all his nine children to college, so he became determined to excel in football. That earned him a scholarship to Northeast Louisiana University, where he graduated in 1971 with a business degree.

Later that year, he was the Falcons' first-round draft pick and spent several years with the team before being sidelined with a knee injury. He was traded to the New Orleans Saints, where he played out his career.

Mr. Profit's introduction to the business world was not as successful as his entry into professional sports. In 1984, a federal judge ordered him to repay more than $639,000, plus interest, loaned to him by the Small Business Administration for a Jilly's rib restaurant in Atlanta that Mr. Profit had sold. The case finally was settled earlier this year.

During those turbulent years, Mr. Profit managed to build CI into a successful company. He often was the guest of President Reagan, and framed invitations to the White House cover his office walls. His political activism in the early 1980s led many to urge him to run for Congress. But he resisted politics and concentrated on CI.

Joe Profit, who was a running back for the Atlanta Falcons in the 1970s, now owns a successful telecommunications company.

Today, the company is his pride and joy. Last year, it moved into a $5 million two-story office building off Live Oak Parkway near Norcross.

Given his success, Mr. Profit said he hasn't lost sight of the work ethic that took him from his hometown into the mainstream of own business. He said he ... things he needed while growing ...

Still, the company is ... he wants it to be. "Success ... and by no means ..." he said.

Courtesy of Gwinnett Business

THE WALL STREET JOURNAL

MARCH 8, 1994

ENTERPRISE

Small Firms Fight to Win Space on Data Superhighway

Effort Focuses on FCC as It Crafts Rules for Auction of Wireless Spectrum

By Jeanne Saddler

Staff Reporter of The Wall Street Journal

WASHINGTON — Small communications companies and entrepreneurs are fighting to make sure that giant competitors don't drive them off the coming information superhighway.

A big step in that fight begins today, when the Federal Communications Commission starts hammering out rules for auctioning pieces of the radio spectrum for personal-communications services — a new way of sending voice, data and video messages. The rules will strongly influence how big a role small firms play in a potential multibillion-dollar market.

Big Fish Maneuver

At stake is the heart of a wireless system that will let businesses and consumers communicate without the land-based wires of the major telephone and cable companies. Giant corporations such as MCI Communications Corp., American Telephone & Telegraph Co. and the regional Bell telephone companies are all maneuvering for places in this wireless system, where they could offer everything from hand-held phones to on-demand video games. Small companies want to make sure that the FCC writes its rules in ways that also give them access to these lucrative new markets.

"This could be like the great land grab in the West, [illegible]," says Joseph Profit, president of Communications International Wireless Inc. [illegible]

Small communications concerns also are pressing to make sure their interests are protected in sweeping telecommunications legislation now moving rapidly through Congress. Their congressional lobbying has already helped small firms to gain an edge in the coming FCC rules on personal-communications services.

Last summer, Congress ordered the agency to devise a system that would aid the industry's small businesses, as well as those owned by women, minorities and

> "This could be like the great land grab in the West," says Joseph Profit, president of Communications International Wireless.

rural telephone companies. And the FCC has already signaled its intention to set aside two sections of the radio spectrum for those companies in its wireless rules.

But small firms say rules to ease their financial burden are the key to whether they will gain a stake in the new industry. When the FCC auctions off the radio spectrum, these firms want to be able to make smaller down payments if they win a bid and to get the right to pay in installments for any spectrum slots won. Another crucial factor will be the order in which the FCC auctions off parcels of the spectrum, because that will make clear which businesses dominate certain regions and could determine whether big and small companies form lucrative alliances.

Small companies got additional assistance from Capitol Hill in January from Sen. Dale Bumpers, the Arkansas Democrat who heads the Senate Small Business Committee. He wrote the FCC in support of its set-aside intentions and called for the extra financial help sought by small firms.

On the other hand, BellSouth Corp. recently wrote the FCC to argue that set asides would lead to "spectrum ghettos," which would decline in value. BellSouth has led the regional phone companies in opposing the set-aside idea.

Alliances to Gain Muscle

Faced with uncertain prospects, small communications companies are forming alliances to gain muscle in the coming FCC auctions. American Wireless Communications Corp., based in Washington, is a [illegible] alliance of small firms that plan to help each other find financing [illegible] expertise as they compete for personal-communications services [illegible].

"We understood quickly that if we wanted to proceed against deep pockets, our most prudent play would be as a coalition of small to medium-sized businesses," says Walter [illegible], president of the alliance, which was formed last fall.

Another consortium, the Small Business PCS Association in Pursola Valley, Calif., aims to devise its own national personal-communications services network by linking small members' expected systems. Robert Kyle, the group's chairman, says the 40-company alliance wants to offer a system in which a call to a subscriber's San Francisco office, for example, would be forwarded to an office the subscriber is visiting in New York.

Both alliances say they worry that the FCC, stung by industry criticism of its recent decision to cut cable-TV rates again, may delay many decisions that it is to begin considering today. The alliances fear the commission may push back the auctions' debut from this summer until possibly the end of the year. The small-business consortiums say such a delay would let cellular phone companies, major potential competitors, update their systems. Personal-communications services are expected to be a threat to the cellular industry because they are based on a different technology that will be cheaper to use.

The FCC already has created controversy in the nascent industry by granting lucrative licenses to four players since last fall. The commission said the four helped to develop the so-called PCS technology. Omnipoint Inc., a small, closely held firm in Colorado Springs, Colo., won the right to offer one of the two data services in the New York City and northern New Jersey area. Cox Communications Inc., the big cable concern, and American Personal Communications, a partnership of medium-sized and big media companies that includes the Washington Post Co., won free licenses to start wireless-data systems in Los Angeles and Washington, respectively. Mobile Telecommunications Technologies Inc., known as Mtel, was granted one of the 11 nationwide licenses.

Because the FCC has granted a preference to some large companies, the agency should help small ones to a greater degree, argues Mr. Profit of Communications International. "The big guys want to keep the old technology as long as possible," he adds. "We want to put the new technology out there and bring the prices down."

The FCC is considered sensitive to the need to ensure that small communications companies can play a significant role in the emerging wireless arena. It's still unclear exactly what rules the commission will adopt to achieve that end.

Enterprise: Small businesses fight to stay on information superhighway — *Page B2*

Courtesy of Wall Street Journal

Minority Business Development Agency

MBDA Gulf Reconstruction Update: First Minority Contract Awarded in Persian Gulf Region

By Donald R. Beaver

Joe Profit Sr. has experienced the kind of all-around success most people only dream about. Today, as president and chairman of the board of Communications International Inc., an international telecommunications systems integrator, his desire and ambition to excel has transcended both the athletic and business fields. Such success in both worlds is unusual.

A former Commerce Department employee, Profit's formula for business success in the telecommunications industry includes a savvy business sense which was key to steering his firm's growth and development during the post-AT&T divestiture. His pioneering efforts in the telecommunications system integration market were instrumental in developing Communications International from a one-state telephone installation and maintenance company to an international, multi-faceted telecommunications corporation, utilizing the latest in communications technology.

His business efforts have culminated with winning the first competitive prime contract awarded to a minority-owned firm in the Persian Gulf reconstruction effort. The company will assist Bechtel International Inc. and Kuwait's government-owned Kuwait Oil Company. Under a multi-million dollar reconstruction contract, Communications International will supply a mobile satellite telecommunications system used in the ongoing oil well firefighting effort in the Kuwaiti desert. The company will design, engineer and install this critical network in support of rebuilding the Kuwaiti oil industry.

Communications International was assisted in competing for this award by the International Trade Administration and MBDA's Gulf Reconstruction Task Force, which provided assistance and support to the company by supplying strategic data and information on opportunities in the Persian Gulf region.

The contract will enable Communications International to provide an earth station linked to a public branch exchange (PBX) at Bechtel's headquarters in Al Ahmadi, in southern Kuwait. This network will support Bechtel's voice, fax and personal computer data terminals in Kuwait, as well as an extensive cellular system homed into the PBX. The company's first-phase contract is for six months, however the contract's renewal could last up to 10 years.

"This contract demonstrates the ability of American small and minority-owned businesses to successfully compete by providing quality-intensive products and services in the international marketplace," said Profit. "We are especially grateful to Secretary Mosbacher and the Commerce Department for their efforts to promote American business overseas."

Profit's desire and ambition to succeed in the business world can be traced

Joe Profit, right, former Commerce Department employee, All American and National Football League star, and successful entrepreneur, discusses [illegible] opportunities for minority business enterprises in the Persian Gulf region with [illegible], left, Executive Director, Pennsylvania Minority Business Development Agency. Profit was a keynote speaker at MBDA's First Annual National Training Symposium held in Washington, D.C., in July.

Page 6 – Commerce People

Courtesy of CII

PEOPLE

Detroit's head zoo keeper in charge appreciates all animals

KHADEJAH SHELBY

Khadejah Shelby is the only Black zoo director in the country; while her job is primarily an administrative one, she's taken on the additional responsibility of educating Black people about careers in the zoo field.

When she was first appointed deputy director of the Detroit Zoo by Mayor Coleman Young in 1982, there was some public criticism because of her lack of animal experience. She didn't know a panther from a pussycat. But with a few years on the job, including a year working on a certificate in zoo management, she has now become quite knowledgeable. There are 120 zoo employees on her staff, most of whom have degrees in either zoology or biology, who care for the animals directly.

As acting director, the 63-year-old grandmother never misses an opportunity to talk to Black children about animal-related careers. She gives priority to answering every Crayola-crayoned query that comes across her desk. "Many of our youngsters are not encouraged to pursue careers at the zoo. There are a number of career options like zoo architecture and animal dentistry," says Shelby. She has also helped develop a zoo management degree program at Wayne State University.

After some involvement with the Black Power Movement in her native Cleveland and New York, she moved to politically exciting Detroit in 1969 and worked to get Young elected as the city's first Black mayor. Under Young's administration she worked with the city's health department and held various positions in city government before being appointed to the zoo post.

"Zoo work has taught me to appreciate all animals," she says, "from snakes, my least favorite, to people." —[illegible]

JOSEPH PROFIT

growing into a major communications giant

As a running back for the Atlanta Falcons and the New Orleans Saints, Joseph Profit, Sr., was used to being tackled by men much larger than himself. When Profit changed careers, leaving the football field for the business field, his competitive attitude propelled him to the top in the telecommunications world.

Profit, 42, is the president and chief executive officer of Communications International, Inc. (CII), an Atlanta-based telecommunications firm that now has more than $100 million in sales and revenues and 300 employees; and thanks to a $50 million contract with the government of war-torn Kuwait, Profit's company will grow even larger. "When I formed the company in June 1978," says Profit, "it was just myself, a secretary and one installer. Initially we only installed small key telephone systems."

Profit was the first person of color to be awarded a contract to help rebuild Kuwait. "We will design, engineer and install a telecommunications network that will provide telephone service, fax machines and all types of electronic information technology, for transmission from the Kuwaiti government and oil fields back to the United States, Europe and the rest of the world."

In 1984 his company began installing telephone centers on U.S. military bases throughout the country. "CII was the first company to set up communications in the desert, during the Gulf war," says Profit, whose telecommunications company developed Operation Phone Home for the soldiers. After the war, Profit and his engineers went looking for business in Kuwait. He went up against giants like AT&T and GTE. "They had all the resources and the financing. We had the labor and the determination. We just decided, on sheer will alone, that we were going to win the contract," says Profit. The low bidder for the contract, CII, won hands down. The multimillion-dollar contract will run from two to five years and add another 40 employees to CII's payroll. Profit says, "CII has become a big player now." —LLOYD GITE

44 ESSENCE FEBRUARY 1992

Courtesy of Essence Magazine

Profit brings Muhammad Ali to Atlanta, Georgia to present the "Muhammad Ali Telephone" designed and manufactured by Profit's Company

THE ATLANTA CONSTITUTION

INSIDE

What's what on your credit report

Panel of authors feels 'taken in'

'Unprecedented' plan, ACOG chief says

Minorities to get piece of Olympic pie

BUSINESS REPORT: ON MINORITIES

Atlanta inventors introducing games

Kuwait picks Atlanta firm

Forum change

Et cetera

People . . .

Courtesy of Atlanta Journal Constitution

Ambassador Andrew Young and Joe Profit at the Ambassador's Office in Atlanta, GA

President Ronald Regan welcomes Joe Profit to the White House

THE WHITE HOUSE

WASHINGTON

June 17, 1986

Dear Mr. Profit:

Pursuant to the provisions of Section 4(b) of the White House Conference on Small Business Authorization Act, I hereby appoint you a delegate to the National White House Conference on Small Business. I am grateful for your willingness to accept this responsibility and I know that you will make a valuable contribution to the work of this White House Conference.

With warm personal regards,

Sincerely,

Ronald Reagan

The Honorable Joseph Profit
3832 Parian Ridge Road
Atlanta, Georgia 30321

Political Field

President Ronald Regan, Ralph David Abernathy and Rev. Hosea Williams
"Ralph and Hosea endorses the election of Ronald Regan"

Honorable Jack Kemp (NFL/ Presidential Candidate and Vice President Nominee) and me.

Team Profit

Perry Thomas, Don Zimmerman, Me, and Rubin Jones
Friends and Teammates for Life!

Joe Reeder, Wanda (my Wife), and Me
at the Army Navy Club in Washington, D.C.

Seeing the Change in my Peers

When I returned to campus the following week, I brought with me a broken and hollow heart. I was depressed all day, every day. If it hadn't been for the change in my peers—from hatred to acceptance—I don't know if I would have survived one more day at that school. However, by the grace of God, my friends and classmates greeted me with loving arms.

My football team embraced me the most. They had all been first-hand witnesses to the terrible night in Hammond, and when they saw my pain, it was obvious that a little bit of it rubbed off on them.

I started thinking about how blessed I was to finally have people who cared about me. It seemed like it was all part of God's timing that my peers began to embrace me as soon as the strongest foundation of my life gave way. I thought back to how they used to welcome me not with open arms, but with closed fists, and how the whole school scared the living daylights out of me. But after all of that began to subside, I realized that none of it mattered anymore. What was done was done. What was in the past was in the past.

Setting the Record Straight

As my college football career progressed, I continued to play well and the team continued to improve. Around that time, talks began that I would be able to make it in the NFL. If you had asked me when I first walked on at Northeast my freshman year, I would have told you that the NFL was the last thing that was on my mind. Back then, I was only concerned about surviving the campus and earning a degree. But then I started playing. In my sophomore year, I set a school record with 884 rushing yards. In my junior year, I set another record with 1,207. In my senior year, I added another 800, and would have likely broken the record yet again if I hadn't been injured for three of the games. I finished with 23 touchdowns to my name, another Northeast record, and I earned all-conference honors in each of my final three seasons. On top of all that, during my senior year I received the conference Athlete of the Year award; I was named an outstanding running back in the Senior Bowl, and I was elected to the Associated Press all-America first team.

By the end of my final season, there was little doubt that I would be able to make it in the NFL—as well as run with the best of them. With the training from my track coach, Bob Grosclose, I was able to shave my 100-yard dash time down to 9.5 seconds—even 9.4 seconds on a good day. At 205 pounds (which was big for that time), I became one of the top prospects in the country, and I decided to enter the 1971 NFL Draft.

Despite all of my accomplishments on campus, though, I found that I was still relatively unknown by a lot of the fans around the country. I was concerned that I would not be drafted as early as I deserved, but Coach White kept encouraging me, "Boy, don't you worry. All that matters is that you get drafted. Once that happens, they'll see that you can play."

Getting Together

Along with football, there were other extracurricular things on my mind. My relationship with Deborah had progressed to the point that we were beginning to discuss a future together. It was a bit unclear what would happen after I graduated. She was still in school and we knew that I would likely be off to another city once I was drafted. With that in mind, I took a leap of faith and asked her to marry me.

It was a bold decision, as we were both still students at the time, and neither of us had a lot of extra time on our hands to devote to one another. But I figured we could make the time. I wanted to start a family at a young age in the same way that my mom and dad had done. I wanted to honor them by continuing their legacy. I wanted the delight of prosperity that they had experienced in the midst of large adversity. My pastor always told me, "A marriage is a partnership that holds incredible powers. When a man and a woman work together in harmony, they can accomplish miraculous things." I took that lesson and ran with it.

Without missing a beat, Deborah accepted my proposal, and we were married soon after. Because of our busy schedules, though, there was no honeymoon. We were married on a Sunday afternoon and we were back in class on Monday morning.

I was riding high after that. The only bad part was that my dad did not get to witness the wedding. It was a sad thing, but I kept myself in good spirits by remembering how proud he was of me when he died. I knew I could keep making him proud by continuing the legacy that he had left behind.

Draft Day

On the day of the draft, I spent the day back home with my family, huddled around the radio. My mom was there with my younger siblings, but I could still feel the emptiness left by my father's absence. Pearl immediately latched onto Deborah, asking her all sorts of random questions about herself and me. She handled it well. I, on the other hand, was a nervous wreck. I sat at the other end of the couch, with my hands folded and my elbows on my knees, and I didn't talk to anyone. I just kept praying to God that it would all be over soon.

Deborah must have seen the anxiety on my face. After only a couple selections in the first round, she said, "Joe, why don't you go take a walk? It might ease your nerves a bit."

"Okay," I said. I got up and left my family behind. I went down to the corner store where I bought a Coke. I wasn't particularly thirsty; I just needed something mindless to do to take away the thoughts racing through my head. What if I got drafted too late? What if I got drafted to the wrong team? I didn't really care which team I went to, as long as the team was focused on success. I just needed a place where I would be able to take care of my family. What if none of that happened?

I really felt like I needed my dad at that moment. I felt lonely. It was hard for me to be catapulted into the future without him behind me, rooting me on. But the Lord had different plans, so I knew I had to deal with them. That's what my dad would have wanted.

I returned home, after only being gone for a few minutes, to a house that was buzzing with excitement. Deborah came running out of the house when she saw me coming. "Joe," she shouted, "You missed it! You got a call from the Jets, but we had to tell them you weren't home!" I couldn't tell why she was so excited. In those days when a team called, you had to answer the phone in person, otherwise you couldn't get drafted. I had already gotten a phone call—well before I had expected it—and I had gone and blown it because I was out of the house.

"That's not good," I said, "I was supposed to be here to pick up the phone."

But she was still smiling, "It doesn't matter, baby! It means you're on their minds!"

I thought about it, and realized that she was right. The thought that I could go as early as the sixth pick was astonishing. I never would have expected that, and I never would have expected what happened next. I heard the phone from inside. My wife and I exchanged glances, but only for a second, because we both bolted for the door.

The rest of my family was inside, practically bouncing off the walls and lifting the house off the ground. My mom had the phone in her hand and she presented it to me like a gift. I took the phone off the receiver, almost fumbling it to the ground in my excitement.

"Hello?" I said.

"May I speak with Joe Profit, please?"

"This is him."

My siblings were jumping on the sofa, as my mom tried to shush them down, mouthing Quiet! He's on the phone! After only a few brief moments, I thanked the man and hung up the phone.

"I'm going to Atlanta." I said. My family erupted in cheers, and started dancing around the living room. A few moments later, I heard my name over the radio broadcast, and that's when it hit me.

I was on my way to the NFL.

The 1971 NFL Draft was not only a special day for me. It was a special day for many of my peers as well, and it was a remarkable day for the record books of small college football programs in the South. Of the first ten overall choices in the NFL draft, none of them came from the big southern schools such as LSU, Georgia, Alabama, and

Texas. Instead, four of the ten came from small schools in Louisiana. Those players were Richard Harris, drafted number five overall by the Philadelphia Eagles out of Grambling; Joe Profit, number seven overall by the Atlanta Falcons out of Northeast Louisiana; Frank Lewis, number eight overall by the Pittsburgh Steelers out of Grambling; and Isiah Robertson, number ten overall by the Los Angeles Rams out of Southern. There were a total of eight selections from Grambling and two from Southern.

When it was announced that "Joe Profit" was chosen by the Falcons as the seventh overall pick in the 1971 NFL draft, the reception was similar to what I had expected. A large portion of the media—both national and local—shrugged their shoulders and said, "Joe who?" I was still an unknown, but I was ready to take Coach White's advice and make myself known. I knew I could do it—all that remained was to do actually do it.

But before I could, I had other things to resolve. I was still in school, and there was much work to be done before graduation. I knew if I didn't finish my degree, my mom would 'whoop' me so badly that I wouldn't run a single yard for the Falcons.

Once I returned to campus though, it was hard to retain focus. I was bombarded by anyone and everyone. People were shouting my name; people were giving me compliments. I couldn't walk down the sidewalk to class without being ambushed by a group of strangers giving their congratulations. It was a stark contrast to my freshman year. The people who had spat on me were now the ones giving me handshakes, hugs and pats on the back.

I realized another thing that Coach White had said had come

true; if I played hard enough, people would come around. Well, come around they did. In the week following my selection to the NFL, the student council voted to celebrate Joe Profit Day—in honor of my struggle through adversity. On February 18th, hundreds of people gathered for the commemorative ceremony. In attendance were my family and friends, my football team, Coach White, my high school head coach, Mackie Freeze, my future head coach for the Falcons, Norm Van Brocklin, and my biggest mentor in life after my father, Mr. Robinson. At the end of the ceremony, Coach White announced that my jersey, #40, would be retired from play, making it the first ever retired number at Northeast.

It was an enormous blessing to have a day in my honor—particularly since it was voted on by the students. When I saw all the people that showed up to celebrate with me, I began to cry. I could only think of how much had changed. At first, I was hated. Now, I was the most celebrated student on campus. Now, my family and friends were no longer afraid to be on the campus. Here they all were, scattered among the white people, embraced as a part of the community. As I thought about it more, I realized that it wasn't a celebration of me. It was a celebration of everyone—a celebration of us all coming together as one entity.

<u>Checking off the List</u>

At long last, I made it to graduation. It was difficult to believe four years had already gone by at Northeast. Looking back to the first time I set foot on the campus—when I nervously walked across the football field and shook hands with Coach Dixie White—it felt like a distant, hazy memory. Now, I was getting ready to walk across a stage, and I still felt the same nerves. But little by little, as I took each step toward my diploma, the memories flipped through my head and I started making check marks of everything I had done. Graduate in four years. Check. I had accomplished so much in my time there. I went through many personal battles on the football field, in the classroom, on the campus and at home. I was tested endlessly. All those nights spent doubting my capabilities, and all those days spent being mocked and shunned and cast out by my peers—they all went by like a whirlwind, but at the time, they seemed to take an eternity. Even though I was mocked and shunned, I stayed with the track and football teams for all four years. Played football in the fall and ran track in the spring. Check. I had even stayed the course with my education. Even when teachers counted me out, I used their hateful words as stepping stones, and worked harder than any of my classmates. Despite all of the roadblocks, I still kept my grades up. Make it on the Dean's List. Check.

I had completed the list. I had done the things I had set out to do at the beginning of college. But looking out into the sea of white faces cheering for me as I walked across the stage into graduation, I couldn't help but smile knowing that I had done even more than I had ever thought possible.

In four years, I went from being the most despised person on campus to the most beloved hero. In four years, I changed the minds of hundreds, maybe thousands of fans, on what it means to respect your fellow human being. In four years, I had changed the minds of my student body, from those who slid their desks away from me to those who now gathered closely around me.

Now I was on my way away from the campus. I was on my way to starting a new family. I was on my way to the NFL, to a world that was much different than a college campus, where people would again know nothing about me or my character. I knew that I could no longer look back on all the things I had done or all the challenges I had overcome. There were new challenges ahead, and I had to be prepared to turn them into stepping stones. I'd be lying if I said it didn't scare me, but I knew what I had done before. I knew I could do anything with hard work and faith. Thankfully, I had been prepared by my family, by my community and by my mentors for my transition to the next field of my life.

DETERMINATION AND RESILIENCY

Pre-Season Pressure

Directly after graduation, my wife and I were forced to adjust to life in Atlanta. The move was overwhelming for several reasons. For one, I had lived my whole life in Louisiana, in a relatively small city. Atlanta was still a southern city, but the size, and consequently the lifestyle, would prove to be drastically different from what I was used to. Second, I had lived my whole life as a poor man. Back in those days, the NFL players weren't earning near the proportions they're earning today, but even so, the salary I anticipated earning was head and shoulders above anything I or my parents had ever made before. And third, my wife was now pregnant with our first child, and I had to do my best to keep the pressure off of her.

But I'm way too far ahead of myself. When my wife and I moved to Atlanta in the summer of 1971, I still had not signed a contract with the Falcons. In fact, I was the longest hold out in Falcons history at the time, and the reason behind it is something I'm truly proud of. Back in those days, the NFL was notorious for paying black players far less than they actually deserved. They had a monopoly on pro football after the merger with the AFL, so most teams could get away with underpaying their players with no fear of repercussions. They figured most of the black players, like me, had grown up poor and would scrape their hands dry for any offer that had zeros in the number. My friend, James "Shack" Harris, who had entered the league two years before me, was making about one-tenth of the salary of his white counterparts despite being a Pro Bowl MVP quarterback. I also knew that teams sometimes offered players cars and jewelry instead of long term financial security. For me, the hold out was a statement of pride. I wanted to let them know that I was different than their average man, that I would not let them push me around. If you ask any worker, from blue collar to white collar, they'll say you must negotiate from a position of strength. Once you agree to a contract, then you can concentrate on your work. I had trouble concentrating on football as long as the negotiations were going on with the Falcons. My dad always taught me to go out and get what I was worth. I knew I was worth more than their offer, so I stood by my decision.

My representative at the time was Billy Brown, a state senator who was on good terms with the coaching staff of the Falcons. He insisted that, much like my friend Shack, the team was offering a substantially small fraction of what I deserved. As early as the day I was drafted, a feud between Mr. Brown and the Falcons ensued, and continued through spring and summer. All the while, I listened to Mr. Brown. I let him do his business, and made sure I kept my mouth shut.

Late in July, when training camp was well under way, I was still without a contract. The fans and media were starting to get restless, mostly at the team and not at me. In the news, there were countless articles comparing me to Gale Sayers, who was in his later days with the Chicago Bears. They said I had the same build, quickness and agility that made Sayers so unique, and that I was destined for similar success.

Naturally, most people began wondering why team management was showing such little support for the player in whom they, the coaches, supposedly had the utmost confidence.

Meanwhile, I was in Chicago with Mr. Brown at the Continental Plaza Hotel. I was getting set to play in the College All-Star Game, a charity game in which the best college seniors faced the reigning NFL champions (in this case, the Baltimore Colts). It was the day of the game when the Falcons' President, Frank Wall, flew out to meet with me and Mr. Brown at the hotel. We entered into negotiations for the final time, and I signed my first contract only two hours before the start of the game. We agreed not to disclose the specifics of the contract, but it was publicized that I was set to make six figures with incentives based on performance. It was one of the most lucrative contracts for an incoming rookie of that time. In the end, the long wait was worth it to me. When I signed that contract, I felt so blessed. I could finally start providing for my family the life that my father had always envisioned.

The first pre-season game had already been played by the time I returned to Atlanta. In fact, I was barely able to strap on my new uniform in time for the next game. But it didn't matter—at last I was ready to play. And when I did, I hit the field like thunder. Within the second pre-season game I began to turn heads with my quick legs and nimble feet. Right out of the gate, the fans were happy to see that I was for real—that I really did have potential to be the next Gale Sayers. Now when somebody said "Joe who," it was only because I blew by them so quickly that they had no time to learn my last name.

I was reminded again of Coach White, and his words to me on

the field, "That's how you change attitudes, Son. Good work."

By the end of the pre-season, I had gained more yards than any other Falcon despite joining the team later than anyone else. To me, it appeared that the time off had done me well. I was not bitter toward the team or anyone involved. I was just happy to finally be on the field, and to once again start proving myself in every way possible.

The only person who was still unhappy with me was, unfortunately, the most important person I had to answer to—my head coach, Norm Van Brocklin. Coach Van Brocklin was a former quarterback for the Rams and the Eagles, and he had just been inducted into the Pro Football Hall of Fame earlier that year. When he became a coach, he gained a reputation as a no-nonsense man. He was hard to approach, and even harder to get to like you. Most of all, he was vocally critical about my hold out. He claimed that I was asking for too much money, and he stayed bitter with me, even after I showed the world that I was worth it.

During practice, he would openly criticize me in front of everyone else on the team. Whenever I would drop a pass, he would pick up the ball, shove it in my gut and shout, "We're not giving you a boxcar full of money to drop passes, Joe!" He would insult me any way he could. Most of the times, the drops weren't even my fault, but he would still find a way to make it look like they were. I quickly became the scapegoat for every pass that was dropped, every block that was missed, and every play that went away. If Coach ever had a canker sore, it was most likely my fault too.

In spite of the disdain he showed for me, I continued to garner the appreciation of the fans and the media. The positive attention made it harder for Coach Van Brocklin to treat me as a scapegoat, but that only meant he had to do it more quietly.

Growing Along with my Roots

By that time, Deborah and I had moved out of our apartment and into a three-story home on the upper side of Atlanta. The house was huge, like a cavern, but I grew anxious in anticipation that it would soon be filled by my first child.

Meanwhile, the rest of my family was cheering me on back at home. More than anything, they were excited that they could see their baby on television. I got so many calls from them I thought they would never stop. I got a call from my mom one night after a game, and she was nearly in tears.

She said, "I knew you were special from the moment I held you in my arms, son. I can't tell you how proud of you I am. You stuck with it, through everything, and you've made us both proud." Just hearing those words made my eyes start to water. I knew my dad was still with all of us, and I knew he would be proud of me as well—mostly for never giving up.

It's Never too Early to Dip into the Next Field

If there's one core value that's overlooked in the world of business education, it's the art of making connections and building relationships. The old adage says "It's not what you know, but who you know." I would not go so far as to deface the value of intellectual knowledge, but the value of personal connections is not to be underestimated. My good friend James "Shack" Harris, who played pro football for 13 years, used to come home from the pros in the summers. He would tell all of us in the neighborhood, "When you make it big, always get to know the managers, the owners and the executives. These people are your foundation for success later on." After Shack left the field, he worked his way through the ranks and currently serves as Senior Personnel Executive for the Detroit Lions.

I feel with my upbringing, with my mom and dad and people like Mr. Robinson always urging me toward success, that I was conditioned to have this mentality. So when I started my rookie year workouts with the Atlanta Falcons, I naturally shifted into business mode and began establishing my network. The owner of the Falcons at the time was Rankin Smith, one of the 'top dogs' of business in Atlanta and in the entire South. Along with running the Falcons, Smith ran the Life Insurance Company of Georgia, and he took an active part in the Georgia community by donating and raising millions of dollars in charity work. In short, Mr. Smith worked as a template for how I envisioned my life after football. I yearned not only for football fame, but for a true, healthy mixture of financial success and community service. I knew that Mr. Smith could work as more than a template, though. He could actually help me achieve that kind of success.

I began to pursue Mr. Smith after practice. In a way, it kind of felt like school again; where I would finish with football, clean up, then go do my homework. In this instance, I would finish with football, clean up, and then go wait outside Mr. Smith's office. Mr. Smith was an incredibly busy man, so I would sit there for hours each week, flipping through old magazines, staring at the wall or just twiddling my thumbs to pass the time. Sometimes I would get in a quick word with him on his way out the door, but sometimes he never came out at all. It seemed pointless to any of the onlookers. My teammates were all eager to get home at the end of the day, to rest and prepare for the next day's practice. Sometimes my coach would see me, sitting there in the same chair having made no progress toward a meeting, and he would say, "Give it up, Joe. Your job is to play football."

I respected my coach, and I agreed with him that my job was to play football, but I also knew that I had more than football on my horizon. Recurrently, I saw my teammates and coaches go home in the evening, but I stayed dedicated.

One day while waiting, one of the janitors cleaning the lobby noticed me. He motioned with his broom over in my direction, "I've seen you here before, son," he said, "What are you doing outside Mr. Smith's office every day?"

"Well, I want to talk to Mr. Smith."

"About what?"

"About his business. I'm hoping to start my own business one day, and I want to ask Mr. Smith for advice."

He rested his chin on the end of his broomstick, and then said, "You're a football player, though. You're a rookie. What're you thinking about business for?"

I stood with my principles and said, "I know I'm young, but I also know that a lot of people like me lose their lives once they're done with football. I'm different. I've got ambition, and I don't want any of that to happen to me."

The janitor studied me. It seemed like there was some sympathy in his eyes. I'm sure that to him, a lot of the football players seemed washed up, with loads of money that they didn't earn or deserve. But I was different, and I'm sure he saw it in me. After a few seconds, he popped his head up off his broom and motioned for me to come follow him. I glanced at Mr. Smith's door. I realized that, much like the other days, it probably wasn't opening anytime soon, so I got up and followed the man I had just met. He took me a short distance down the hallway until we came to a corner. With his broom, he pointed to a door halfway down the near wall. It seemed like a fairly plain door, and I thought at first that it was more than likely his janitor closet. "Try waiting over there," he said. I looked at him, confused, and then he added, "It's Mr. Smith's back entrance. Whenever he's really busy, that's where he'll go."

The janitor kept a real stern face, but after a moment, he broke down and smiled. I smiled in return. Then he just patted me on the back and said, "Best wishes, young man."

That very day, I caught Mr. Smith as he left through the back door. I said, "Mr. Smith, can I have a word with you for a moment?"

He looked startled that I had found his secret escape door, "Joe! What are you still doing here?"

"I've been waiting to talk to you. Sorry if this is bad timing."

"Well, I'm sorry Joe, but it is bad timing. It's been a long day and I just don't have the time right now."

I told him that I understood, but just because I understood didn't mean that I was going to have a change of heart. I kept waiting outside his office. Every day. Up to that point in my life, I had learned a lot about diligence. I knew that there are certain barriers in our lives that look impassable—like playing in a stadium full of people who hate the color of your skin, or standing tall before your boss and asking for a favor—but once you challenge those barriers; you'll look back on the tail end and realize they weren't all that big to begin with. The hardest part is the first step.

When Mr. Smith finally saw the ambition and diligence I displayed just by showing up every day on schedule, he broke down and let me into his office.

"Alright, Joe. I've seen your sad self out there in the hallway every single day. What's it going to take to get rid of you?" He joked, flashing a polite smile.

I shook his hand and took a seat opposite his desk. "Mr. Smith," I said, "I've been studying your work—not just with the Falcons, but with Life of Georgia as well. I'm hoping to start my own business one day, and I was hoping that you could help me get started."

He looked perplexed, "Get started? Joe, you're playing football for us this fall. Take it from me; I don't think it's the right time to be starting a business."

"Well, I don't want to do it now. I want to give all I can on the football field, but once that's done, I want to be able to give it my all in the business field."

He grinned at my play on words. He had seen my ambition; he had seen my diligence, and now he saw my sincerity. "Joe," he said, "I think we can help each other out."

Mr. Smith agreed to let me be a spectator at the office. He said I could meet with the lower-level employees and learn how they do their business. At the time, I was hoping for more, but I was thankful for the opportunity. The very next day, I came prepared with a binder, notebook and pencil. I told Mr. Smith that I was eager to take notes and learn anything I possibly could about his business. He seemed intrigued.

Keep in mind that when I tell you to make connections, they should be more than just superficial ones. Often we can get in the mindset that we just need to meet the right people, and then use them up until they are no longer any value to us, but this is the wrong way to go. The connections and relationships you make should work both ways. You should be looking to gain something, but you should also be looking to give something. You should not be selfish. People at the top of the business chain won't fall for any bull, and they can tell a selfish heart from a selfless one.

The Injury: Learning to Cope with Defeat

The success I had on the field in the pre-season did not stop once the regular season began. By the first game, I had made my mark and people all around had noticed. I started getting more playing time, and I was receiving most of the snaps on the team.

Soon, though, I took a blow to my knee that would prove to set more than my knee off track. All I did was make an inside cut to run around a blocker, but the guy behind me grabbed onto my leg and pulled me to the ground. A shot of pain went through my body, so strong I couldn't believe I held onto the ball. Actually, it may have been the only reason I did. I gripped the ball tight like a soldier biting a bullet. When I landed hard on the turf, I clutched my knee. I knew something was wrong.

The injury turned out to be a tear in my ACL. In today's game, an ACL tear is a slap on the wrist. Back then, in 1971, it was a death sentence. While I was lying on the grass, I saw a large stretch of field ahead of me leading toward the end zone. That's how it was in the game, and that's how it felt in my life—like I had failed to finish the race that was set before me. And it all happened in the fourth game of the season.

After the injury, I sat in the hospital a lot. I was confined to a bed, and imprisoned by the new cast around my leg. Suddenly, the media in Atlanta were turning on me, saying things like, "He didn't show up to training camp. He didn't work out his body. He wasn't conditioned for the NFL." The fans were even less forgiving. I didn't believe any of that stuff was true—I knew I was conditioned and I knew I had the numbers early in the season to back it up—but that didn't stop people from professing their opinions. Because of that, I became very angry.

I started looking for a place to point a finger. I became frustrated with the doctors, and I was stubborn with my wife. I didn't want her to see me in my weakness. I was a family man now, and if I couldn't provide for my family, I would be a failure, and I couldn't let anyone think I was a failure.

I was hard on myself, too. My subconscious would try to convince me that I could have prevented the injury. "You could have trained harder." It would say. "You could have stretched better." "You could have cut right instead of left." These thoughts entered my brain in the long, lonely nights in the hospital bed.

Now, anyone who's had to spend an extended period of time in a hospital knows that it loses its appeal after . . . about three minutes. The walls become boring, the food becomes bland and the world as a whole becomes stale. For me, I had to spend six weeks there. It was awful. I would have rather spent six weeks as the house guest of Dr. Garrett.

By the third week, I had enough—not of the hospital, but of my own attitude. I was tired of being angry all the time and I realized that sulking in self-pity wasn't going to heal my knee. One night, while sitting alone in my bed, I folded my hands and started praying.

"Lord," I said. I was a little rusty. Lately the only words I had sent up to the sky were the kind that didn't belong there. I cleared my throat and started again, "Lord, I know how I've been acting lately. I know my attitude has been wrong. You say that everything happens for your own will, but Lord, why are you doing this to me? All the roadblocks you've put me through, I've turned them into stepping stones and now I finally get somewhere that feels like an accomplishment, and you take it away."

I stopped right there. I listened to what I had just said. I realized that I still had the wrong attitude. I was trying to blame God for everything that had happened to me, but I was looking at it the wrong way.

From that hospital bed, I looked backward at my life and realized that each one of those stepping stones really did make me grow. Now, I was looking at one more opportunity, and I was throwing it aside. I realized I should have been thankful for the injury because it gave me one more chance to grow! I decided from then on that I would let Him take the reins and do what he had planned for me. I would try my hardest to get back on the field, but if it didn't happen, I'd let him take me down a different path, and I would trust that I would be okay.

During rehabilitation, it felt as though I were a baby learning to walk again. My doctors treated me that way, too. I remember my primary trainers, Dr. James Funk, Jr. and Jerry Rhea, watched my progress on a regular basis, and after the first few weeks of walking with a limp, Dr. Funk told me I'd be lucky if I ever lost that limp. He tried to look sorry, and when I told him I had a five-year plan for my future in the NFL, he barely caught himself from laughing. I didn't let that news get me down. I figured just like in football when the media was against me, I could stomp over his low expectation and show him that I wasn't an average Joe.

I continued to pray. I kept my wife in my room with me, and we would pray for hours on end. It became my daily ritual. It was my only escape from the isolation of my bed, and the Lord was my only safe haven. Even though the outlook was grim, I was determined to keep my faith like my mother always advised me.

The Off-season doesn't have to be Downtime

The Falcons' season continued, while I recuperated on the sidelines. I was finally out of bed and I was walking around, but I still brought my crutches and my limp with me everywhere I went. Without me in the lineup, the team went on to record seven wins, six losses and one tie. It was the Falcons' first ever winning season, but it wasn't enough to bring them into the playoffs. For the team, and for me, the offseason started early.

When there's no more football left, it can be tempting to sit back and do nothing. That's how a lot of players go about it. Then, when July rolls around the next year, they decide they'd better get in shape, and spend a few weeks training hard.

Not me, though. I worked hard all year round, trying to rehabilitate my knee in time for the next season. By January, I could tell it was getting a lot better, but there was still a way to go.

I also started working hard in other endeavors of my life. Deborah continued to grow with our first child, who was expected in the coming weeks. This was a blessing to us both, but with my career on the field in question, the news brought a financial burden to the family. I realized quickly that I needed another source of income. This made sense in the short term, as I had a lot of downtime while rehabilitating my knee. But it also made sense in the long-term. Even if I were to play football again, the simple fact was that I would not be in the league forever. I decided I needed to get a foot comfortable in the business field while I still had one on the football field.

In line with what Shack had told me, I had started talking to Rankin Smith more and more. I would meet him at his office off-campus, at the Life of Georgia headquarters, where I would wait for him outside his office just like I had done before. Every time he would see me, he'd ask how my leg was doing, and I would respond, "Strong enough to catch up with you." While I wasn't a fool—I could tell he was getting frustrated with my persistence—I was determined to keep in contact with him. I started going there every day, even if it was just to get a passing conversation with him.

On one of those occasions, I caught Mr. Smith right at the back door of the building. He stopped and said, "Joe Profit, my number one draft choice! You looking to come in here with your playbook ?"

"No sir. I'm really looking for a job," I said.

He looked shocked, like I had been hiding in a cave for the past year. "Joe, I told you; I got you a job! You play football. How are you going to handle a job in a place like this?"

He meant it as a rhetorical question, but I surely didn't take it as one. (That's another tip I have for you—whenever you can, keep as many doors open as possible. Your doors are your connections, but they're also your opportunities. When you close a door, you lose an opportunity).

"Sir," I said, "I know I play football, but I'm not just a football player."

He cocked an eyebrow. I continued, "In reality, I'm a husband, a son and a father. I'm a hard worker, I'm an intellectual. I'm a man of character and I'm a man of determination. I'm a leader, not a follower. A driver, not a passenger. In my life I've been kicked down in the mud, but I've gotten back up and made myself smell like roses. I'm an honest, loyal and decent young man." I paused to take a breath. He seemed impressed, but he didn't know where it was all going. I finished, "But only after all that, am I a football player."

Mr. Smith took a moment to study me. I stood my ground, firm and tall. Then he said, "I didn't have you pegged for an entrepreneur."

"We're all entrepreneurs," I said, "but I'm better than anyone else I know."

He smiled. "Joe, I'm glad you're determined as you are, but the truth is we don't need any help right now." He turned to push the door open, but I stepped in his way. He looked down, "Leg's looking pretty good."

"I want to see how your business truly works. The higher-ups—I want to see how they work," I said. I was done playing games. This time I wanted results. "I just want to sit in with you—watch, listen and make observations. I want to learn the way of the businessman."

At that moment, I could tell he knew I was sincere. Maybe I showed the same promise that he once did—I don't know. But he took his hand off the door, let it close, and looked me in the eye. "You're not a football player."

"No sir. Not just a football player."

He let out a laugh. He offered a hand for me to shake, and I gave him the most firm, manly handshake of my life to that point. "Joe," he said, "You're real good. So here's what I'm going to do. I'll introduce you to my managers and let you sit in on a few of the meetings. Only as an observer. A fly on the wall. Anything more than that, I can't help you right now."

I looked back at him and said, "That's all I needed to hear." After that, I started going to work at Life of Georgia, even though I didn't technically have a job.

It was a little awkward at first. A lot of people at Life of Georgia wondered what I was doing in a place of business like theirs, and I guess I couldn't blame them. I was a young, black professional athlete who walked around on crutches. I did a good job of keeping attention away from myself, though. As Mr. Smith had promised, he let me sit in with his men during the manager meetings.

One valuable lesson I learned early on is that you need to separate your business from all other parts of your life. You cannot let it be invasive; otherwise your business will become who you are, rather than a small part of you.

I still have a memory of our first meeting. Mr. Smith brought me with him into the board room where there were several men seated at a long table. When we entered the door, each of them turned to meet his eyes, and then they all immediately set their eyes on me. It was an uncomfortable feeling. I had met some of them already, but still didn't know them very well, and as I was stranded in the field of their gaze, I started to feel like I didn't belong.

During the meeting, these guys continually got into heated arguments. I don't even remember what they were about now, but I remember how fiercely they fought for their ideas. Watching them pass around papers and sprawl out charts and figures on the table, these guys looked more like they were plotting out a war zone battle. Throughout the whole meeting, I didn't say a word. I just sat and watched the squabbling before me, far too afraid to interject, and far too intimidated to make my voice heard.

Too quickly, the meeting ended. It was like the spontaneous passing of a storm. The men shook hands in parting, gathered their things, and then what happened next blew me away—they went out for dinner with each other. As the rookie in the room, I was asked to join in, so of course I took the opportunity.

When we got to the restaurant, I sat down, and the first thing I did was take out my pen and paper, ready to be immersed in more charts and figures. However, when I did that, I noticed that there were none to be found. All I could see were glasses of drinks and smiling faces. It was like they had taken their papers and thrown them out the window. Once we were out of the business setting, it was a friendly atmosphere. They bought each other drinks, told jokes, and even got me involved in their conversations.

In the parking lot after dinner, I asked Mr. Smith, "How do you do that—you know—how do you argue tooth-and-nail with each other, then go out and act like none of it ever happened?"

He smiled, "That's the beauty of business, Joe. It's just a game. Once it's over, none of it really matters anymore."

That night taught me importance of keeping your business in your business. This would help me later on when I started running my own businesses. It would help me be a better family man, where I would be there every night for my wife and children without bringing charts and figures to the dinner table. It helped me be a better person outside of the office, so that I could have even the most stressful day at work, then come out and be at peace. This lesson made it easier for me to succeed simultaneously in business and in life.

By the following summer, I was off my crutches, walking and even running on a regular basis. It was still difficult to tell, though, whether or not I would be able to make it back on the team for the 1972 season. My knee felt fine while training, but training and playing were two different things. I still didn't know if I had regained my full form, and I wouldn't be able to test myself until I was able to knock pads with another player.

In the meantime, I continued attending the board meetings at Life of Georgia. I had gotten to know some of the other managers, and just as importantly, I had begun to assimilate myself with the culture surrounding the business. I had begun to feel more comfortable in the board room, and even had the courage to speak my mind or ask a question once in a while.

It was all a dream come true for me. I was making connections in the business world, which helped me finally realize how right my friend Shack Harris had been. Get to know the executives of your team. Well, I surely had gotten to know Rankin Smith during that time. I had come to appreciate his work, and he had come to appreciate my work ethic. One day, I built up the courage and caught up to him after a meeting.

"Sir, would you have a minute to step aside?" I asked.

It seemed he already knew my motive. "You're looking for a job again, son?"

"Yes sir." I nodded, keeping my eyes firmly on his.

"Well, I guess I knew it would happen eventually."

"Sir," I said, "I feel like I've been working hard these past few months. You've seen me in action. You've seen how I'm a quick learner and a good observer. To be honest, I think it would be a crime for you not to hire me."

He sighed, and then ran his hand across his face. He wasn't looking at me anymore, but it was still a good sign that he was taking his time—it meant he was actually considering me. Finally, he said, "Joe, you're one of the best I've seen. To be honest, I think it would be a crime not to hire you too." He smiled, and then offered out his hand. "We just recently got a position open in public relations. It's not the board room, but, well, like you said, you're a quick learner. I'll look forward to seeing you there tomorrow."

The best part of the new job was regaining my financial security. My new child was on the way, which made it all that much more of a blessing to not be living in doubt on a daily basis, at the total discretion of a ligament in my knee. It was comforting to know that I had two jobs—albeit for the same boss—that I could lean on for support.

While I continued to go to work at Life of Georgia, I kept strong in my physical rehabilitation with the help of Jerry Rhea. Anyone with a long-term leg injury can testify that the first time you're able to run again, you feel more like you can fly. This is how I felt. I was spreading my wings and letting them soak in the sun. By the early summer, there was virtually no pain left in my knee. I was doing my normal training on a daily basis, I was running laps around my neighborhood, and on top of all that, I could cut and spin with a confidence I had not felt in almost a year.

I reported to training camp as scheduled at the end of July. By that time, I was ready to hit the field and put my knee to the test.

Although the fans and media were a bit skeptical of my ability, they welcomed me back warmly. The common perception at that time was that players returning from an ACL tear were "never one hundred percent." They continued to hope that I could be the answer to their prayers—the next Gale Sayers. By comparison, Sayers—who had just announced his retirement from the Bears—had suffered the same knee injury early in his career. What kept me going was the knowledge that he had rebounded and gained over a thousand yards the following year. Coincidence or not, it was a comforting fact.

Returning to the Field

Coming off the injury, my biggest roadblock was Coach Norm Van Brocklin, who still resented me because of the prolonged salary negotiation. Even though he and everyone he knew had seen what I was capable of, he appeared to be impenetrable, and an insurmountable stepping stone that could not be conquered. No matter how hard I worked or how big a play I made, it seemed like he refused to budge.

When our eyes met on the first day of training camp—for the first time in months—his face turned to a grimace, as if he were disgusted that I was still around. "Joe Profit," he said, "I didn't think we'd see you back here so soon."

He said 'so soon', but I figured he was hoping he wouldn't see me back there, period. It didn't surprise me that we had a few new running backs in training camp that year. It seemed that Coach Van Brocklin was going to try anything he could to prove to me and the media that I wasn't worth the boxcar full of money. But I knew that he was on a short rope. The fans wanted more of me, which meant there was more pressure than ever for him to give in.

I could have thought of a clever response, but I didn't feel like it would have accomplished anything. I just wanted to let my legs do the talking. While looking Coach in the eye, I threw on my shoulder pads and ran out onto the field.

It was a few days in training camp before we did full-contact. The whole time, I was jittering to get back into the game. I mentioned how running for the first time can make you feel like you're flying—well, when you line up against a defense of eleven men for the first time in ten months, you feel like you're soaring through the universe.

At last, the time came for my first full-contact drill.

Eagerly, I took the ball from the quarterback. As soon as it molded to my hands it was no longer a ball, but a friend that I hadn't seen in a long time. I took that friend and I embraced him tightly to my side, clamping down hard so he would never abandon me again. Immediately, I felt a warm sensation pulsing through my body. The reunion was heavenly.

Then again, there was no time to engage in sentimental reverie, for less than a second later I was reintroduced to another old friend of mine. His name was cold, hard dirt, and his welcoming wasn't so warm. I found myself pasted to the ground a few yards behind scrimmage, only an instant after the first play had begun. I heard a whistle blow somewhere far off, but I couldn't tell which direction it came from. As I looked upward from behind my face mask, all I could see was the sky. Pure, blue sky.

There was no pain in my leg.

I got up and dusted myself off. It was only then that I realized everyone else had been holding their breath. I looked around, and then shook out my leg to get the blood back and running. I motioned that I was okay. I turned to the sidelines and I saw Coach Van Brocklin. He just stared at me; from behind his sunglasses - his eyes were expressionless stones. Then I smiled.

My dad always told me that there are no plateaus in any walk of life. You can either go up or go down, get better or get worse, but you never stay the same. When we started training camp that year, I was out there for only one reason, and that was to prove to myself that I could get better. By then, it wasn't about the fans, the media or the money. It was me testing myself and my willpower.

The opening preseason game took place against the Miami Dolphins. When I took to the field for the first time in almost a year, I let the lights of the stadium soak in. They were warm, like a day at the beach. At that moment, I knew I was home where I belonged. But I had no idea the fury that I would unleash in the coming weeks.

Midway through the third quarter, Coach Van Brocklin begrudgingly put me into the game—a sheer statement that he would appease the media and the fans, at least for the preseason. But I showed up to play, and I would make sure everyone knew I was a regular season starter. In just over one quarter, I ran for 60 yards. Not bad, but I was just getting started. The next week in New England, I received more playing time after Coach was pressured by my previous performance. In that game I amassed 89 yards. We lost both of those contests, but in the final preseason game, we would demonstrate that we could win—and win big.

Coach started me for the first time that year. He really had no other choice, as I was leading the team in rushing yards and touchdowns. The fact that he hadn't started me earlier made many of the fans and media start to raise their eyebrows.

Well, for all I cared, they could keep their eyebrows raised because that night I broke out a 169-yard, two-touchdown performance—the best ground game of any Falcon in history, regular season or pre-season. If not for a penalty late in the game, I would have added another 42-yard score, giving me over 200 yards and a third touchdown.

It was a stunning reversal from my regular season of the previous year, where I had gained a total of ten yards in four games. Even though I was sprouting a year later than I had hoped, I was finally playing some serious football.

By the end of the preseason, I was by far the team's leading rusher, and there was absolutely no excuse for Coach Van Brocklin to keep me on the sidelines. The fans were calling for me, and I was wholeheartedly ready to answer.

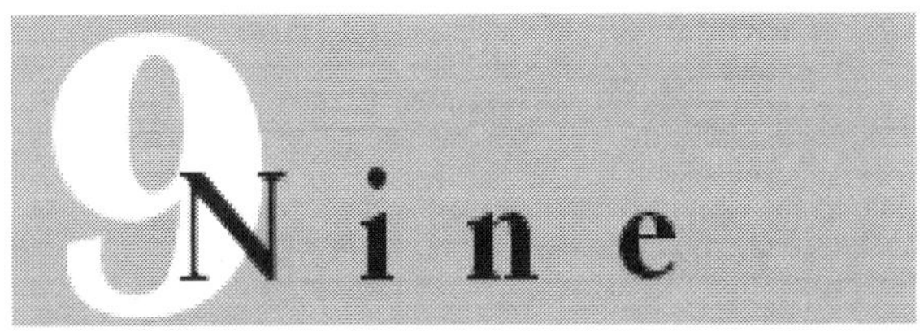

TWO FIELDS AT ONCE

Two Fields at Once

Off the field, I had more matters to tend to. My first son, Joseph Profit, Jr., had just been born, and my wife and I were trying to ration out our time we could spend together, and I was trying to balance the two jobs that I had. My position at Life of Georgia was steady and helpful, but with the arrival of the football season, it no longer allowed me to spend the time with my family that I needed.

I decided eventually that I would have to take a risk. I humbly told Mr. Smith at Life of Georgia that I could no longer keep the position he had so generously given to me. I thanked him for helping me learn and experience so much about business. It truly was a blessed time that set the stage for the business I would conduct later.

However, I didn't have to wait long for my business debut. Immediately after resigning from my position at Life of Georgia, I acquired the rights to start my own International House of Pancakes restaurant. My wife and I felt that it was the right move. By owning a restaurant, we would be able to stay involved with our business, yet hire managers and employees to assist us along the way. Most importantly, it provided us with a fallback plan. My salary with the Falcons was plenty, but it was only around as long as my knee stayed healthy. My ACL injury was a blind side hit to my family and me, and I couldn't risk having it happen again without a plan in place.

Of course, the work was still not easy by any means. Starting a business was a big step, especially while I was still playing football every week. Though I had a trusted team of employees, the workload called for my presence at random hours of the day. Sometimes I would find myself showering off after football practice, then jumping in my car and heading over to IHOP where I would work until night, then go home, sleep and get ready to repeat the same routine the next day.

If there was one thing I had learned growing up, though, it was the payoff of a good work ethic. Back when I was making four dollars per day in the cotton field, I learned to work hard now for a better payoff later, and I applied that same principle to my business.

Setting a Deep-Fried Example

Even though the work was hard, business began booming quickly. It wasn't long before I had enough money to branch out further. Later that year, I was able to open my first Burger King in downtown Atlanta. For me, this was a special occasion that transcended entrepreneurship. Long ago, as a child in my own hometown, I was thrown out of the Burger Chef restaurant that refused to treat blacks and whites equally. At long last, I was able to have a restaurant of my own that sold hamburgers to everyone regardless of their race—and they were all able to come in through the same entrance, too. Shortly after my Burger King opened, I looked up the small chain of Burger Chef Restaurants in Monroe, and found out that they had gone out of business long ago. I was slow to be joyful at the downfall of another business, but in that instance I felt like the better man had won.

As my restaurants began to pick up steam, there was a large draw of attention from the Atlanta community and media. People were intrigued by the fact that their number one draft choice had set up a restaurants in their city, and a lot of people were happy that I had begun to immerse myself in the community in general.

A local news station called one day and asked about running a bit on my story. The team came down to my first Burger King restaurant downtown and got some footage, then asked me questions about my life and my upbringing, but they seemed most interested in my football career and my recent business success outside of football. I told them, among other things, that I was the first black person to own an IHOP, and I was one of the most successful Burger King owners in the state.

As much as I was proud of what I had done from a racial standpoint, though, there was a part of me that felt it wasn't that important. The fact was that I was a businessman who happened to be black, and people were making it out to be like a physical handicap, or something of the sort. I didn't want it to be that way. I was more focused on the business aspect, and that's what I'm most proud of, because I feel I really made an impact.

How, you may ask, can a man make an impact on his community through a restaurant chain? I did it the same way I had been taught my whole life: by setting an example. I employed a lot of teenagers and young adults in Georgia, and a lot of them grew up in places just like Lake Providence and Monroe. They didn't have a lot of money, and they were working for the same reasons that I worked with cotton as a kid. I noticed that a lot of them shared the same tragedy of low expectations that plagued the poorer parts of America, so I tried to be the one to show them that there was a way out of that cycle.

I quickly learned that it wasn't enough to just be there and look important. Nobody would have given a care if I had showed up in my white collar each morning and stood on a podium while they went along flipping burgers. I knew I had to flip burgers with them. Sometimes I would show up at Burger King to open and stay there until close, and I never spent that time hiding behind a desk in a back room. I went up to the grill and stood alongside the young workers. Sure, the work was mundane, and sure, I got grease stains all over my shining white collar, but none of that mattered. I was there first and foremost to show the youth the importance of hard work. When I stood right beside them flipping burgers, they could tell that I cared about my work.

Sometimes I think that people are not humble enough because they're on such a high rung of the business ladder. They look down, notice the people below them and think, "Why should I associate with them? I've worked my way out of those low rungs and I've earned the right to stay up here."

Well, that's true that you may have earned the right, but you're a fool if you think you're contributing to society by taking yourself out of society. So get down from your rung and help the people climb with you.

But you may say, "Joe, I'm too low on the ladder! There's nobody below me! Who am I supposed to help?" You need to quit telling yourself these lies. There are always, always, always people that look to you for an example. If you're so low on the ladder, it means that there are a lot of other people right next to you. Do them a favor and show them what it means to work your way to the top.

I hold this to be true for any endeavor, whether its work, sports, hobbies or even just as a member of society. We all need to live as an example for others. Remember, it's all about expectations, and if you're living life like someone who belongs on the low rung, then not only do you deserve to be there, but you're telling everyone else that you expect them to do no better.

Feeling the Pressure

While I continued to climb up the rungs in the business field, I slowly climbed the rungs on the football field. I continued to rise without a plateau, just like my dad had said. I worked hard in practice and impressed the onlookers, including the local media, which ran articles about "The Joe Profit we've all been waiting for."

My statistics were improving, though my knee was still not back to its full 100%. I remember trying to hide it from the others—the players, the coaches, the fans and the media. I would do my best to not let them see my pain. If I got tackled and took a blow to my knee, I would mask my face as though nothing was wrong at all. During our two-a-day practices, I put a lot of strain on my knee, and I admit that I was a little bit worried it would give out.

But my worries were eased once the regular season started. The practices were shorter and more focused on football rather than strength and conditioning. Since I had done so well in the pre-season, there was less of a burden, which made it a little easier to concentrate on my individual growth. But I knew that the burden was only off as long as I could continue to play and play well.

No Way to Change his Mind

As opening day approached, I felt a sense of rebirth. I couldn't believe that I was finally going to play in a regular season game once again. Every step I took in my uniform felt like a miracle, and I owed it all to the Lord.

We marched into Soldier Field on September 17th to face the Chicago Bears. In the week leading up to the game, the Chicago faithful became well aware that the media was comparing me to Gale Sayers, and, naturally, they didn't take kindly to the notion that someone from another team was trying to replace their legend. Well, I certainly wasn't trying to do anything of that sort. My goal was just to play football. So I shrugged it off and kept myself focused on the game. I was feeling confident and so were the rest of the Falcons. We were coming off our huge preseason win in Cincinnati—a game in which each one of our teams showed the promise that they had lacked all of last year.

We led the Bears 31-7 at halftime. The team was continuing its momentum from the previous game, but I had only managed to gain a humble 25 yards. I heard a lot of taunts from the fans whenever I ran, but I kept my helmet on, and I kept my mind focused.

"Just score one more," Coach Van Brocklin had told us at halftime, "Get one more touchdown and the Bears are done."

Two minutes into the second half, we had made it to the Bears' 44 yard line. On second down, Coach called a simple running play—a dive up the middle—with the ball put in my hands. I lined up behind our quarterback, Bob Berry, and I scanned the field in front of me. Across the way, on the other side of the line, stood one of the meanest men in football—Dick Butkus. A mental line I drew in my head led my path straight for his numbers.

The ball was snapped and Bob quickly turned with it in hand. I spread my arms open, but the ball wobbled as it transferred between us. As soon as I regained control, I felt all 250 pounds of linebacker collide with my stomach. I was whipped backward, the ball plummeted to the ground and Dick Butkus fell to cover it up.

It all happened in a fraction of a second. I closed my eyes as the stadium roared, applauding their one remaining superstar for knocking down the lowly "imposter". Someone took my hand and pulled me to my feet, though I don't know who it was. I was only concerned with the turnover.

I met Coach Van Brocklin on the sideline.

"What the hell was that?" He screamed.

"It was a bad exchange." I said.

"Bullshit!" he said, "You fumbled my ball!"

"It was a bad exchange!" I repeated. It was the truth. It was equally my fault as it was my quarterback's, but Coach didn't want to hear any of it. Bob Berry had won the spot of starter in preseason, and he wasn't going anywhere. I, on the other hand, was headed straight to the bench. Coach had finally found the excuse he was looking for all season.

I found myself on the bench from that point on. Every so often, I would be put in the game to gain a yard or two, but only during 'garbage time,' when we were either so far ahead or so far behind that our starters were taken out. As my playing time dwindled, so did my numbers, which made it impossible for me to earn my contract bonus. Somehow, I think Coach was aware of that the entire time.

I began to get very agitated. He kept telling me that he would put me in once my numbers got up, but we both knew that it was a catch-22. If I couldn't play, I couldn't get my numbers up. I began to vent my frustrations openly and honestly to the media, and in turn, they began to rain down on Coach Van Brocklin from all sides. They called him crazy for benching the man that they believed was the answer to their prayers—the same man that had set rushing records in the preseason. But when Coach started hearing that I was bad-mouthing him, it only made matters worse. He quickly informed me of his new policy—a bad publicity policy. The rule was, if a player gave a bad image to the team, Coach had it in his power to fine them. I was slapped with a $1000 fine and told never to speak with the media again. Well, I did keep my mouth shut, but only because there was nothing else to be said. I let the media do the speaking for me. In the second half of that season, I only played in three games, and got the ball once in each of those three games.

I played in two games for the Falcons the following year. In between those games, I claimed my spot on the bench (*they never retired my number, but they could have named a bench in my honor with all the time I spent there*) and I continued to let the media do their speaking. It was obvious that Coach Van Brocklin was under fire, but for some reason that I'll never know, he did not budge. Maybe he just had too much pride.

I called my agent, Billy Brown, early in the season. I told him I felt like a top-tier player stuck with a bottom-tier coach. I didn't like to say it that way, but it was the truth that everyone around me knew full well. Mr. Brown, along with all of Atlanta, was well aware of my frustrations by that time. He asked me what I wanted, and I told him I demanded to be traded. "I don't care where I go," I said, "as long as I don't have to play for Norm Van Brocklin."

"Well, that leaves us with a lot of options," he said, "I'll see what I can do."

Everyone told me that it would be automatic—if you made it to the NFL and kept playing well, you would have a long, productive career. By my third year in Atlanta, I didn't feel that any of that was true. In fact, it felt the exact opposite. But I remembered my dad's words and held to them strong. I kept trying to get better, and I never settled for a plateau.

After spending two more games completely on the bench, I got a call from Mr. Brown. He told me that he had two pieces of good news.

"What are they?" I asked.

"Well," he said, "the first is that we've found you a team." I nearly broke the phone, I clenched it so hard. I breathed a sigh of relief. I was finally going away.

"That's great to hear, Mr. Brown," I said, "So where am I headed?"

"Well, Joe, that's the second piece of good news. The call came from the Saints. You fly to New Orleans tomorrow."

Getting out of Dodge

My wife, my boy and I had to pack up that very night. It was exciting knowing that we would be fleeing the city on that short of notice. I still did not know what I would be doing with my home, let alone my businesses, back in Atlanta, but I trusted the Lord to keep those issues at bay until I had time to deal with them. In the meantime, my family was ecstatic that I was moving home to Louisiana. They would finally be able to go to my games and see them on TV, which was a tremendous blessing.

Monroe, being in the northeastern part of the state, was still a good long hike from New Orleans. Deep down in the bayou, the LSU Tigers reigned supreme in college football, which meant there was a good chance that nobody there would even recognize my name. Still, I felt a comforting sense of home as we touched down at Armstrong Airport just after midnight, completing my speedy and impromptu return home. I remember when I first set foot on the soft Louisiana turf. It felt familiar, like an old friend. The air flooded my lungs with memories from my childhood, working in the fields, playing with my friends and walking the train tracks to the middle of nowhere. Any remaining doubt that this was the wrong place for me was immediately washed away with the wind.

My first three years in Atlanta were, without a doubt, integral to my life. During those three years, I was able to develop as an athlete, an entrepreneur, a husband and a father. I again tested the limits of my willpower and my faith, and I learned that each of those can extend further than the eyes can see with the help of the Lord. I also learned not to hold grudges, because most people were not concerned with me as a human being, and they did not know me on a personal level.

But during that time I also carried an immense burden. For the entirety of the three years, I was subjected to criticism every single day. I had a weight thrown on my shoulders that I was not fit to carry. It was an overwhelming weight, and it persistently knocked me down until I could no longer run. As soon as I left town, the weight was off. I was no longer the Coach Van Brocklin's scapegoat for all of Atlanta's troubles. Now I was free from my athletic past and I was ready to start anew.

I had already traveled to New Orleans once, earlier in the year, in fact. On opening day of the 1973 season, the Falcons dropped into Tulane Stadium for a casual visit. Along the way, they managed to trample over the Saints to a 62-7 victory. I scored one of my only touchdowns for the Falcons that game, and I reckon it may have been enough for the Saints to like what they saw.

But the Saints team itself was a mess. Beginning their seventh year in the NFL, they were struggling to gain any notoriety in the league, and even a fan base at home. It wasn't long before the Saints became the "Aints" of football infamy.

In the middle of the pre-season, the Saints fired their head coach, J.D. Roberts, after a poor string of losses. Head coach John North took over with almost no time to prepare. There was chaos throughout the team, and as a result there was no chemistry between the players. They had essentially been left in the trash like a tattered rag.

The one good thing that came from it all was Archie Manning. With all the commotion surrounding the team, Archie seemed to have a gift for keeping a level head (as long as it wasn't being pummeled into the turf by a defensive lineman). He was the only man fit to be the leader of that disheveled team, and on top of it all, he was a southern boy. We grew up on different sides of the tracks, for sure, but we were able to relate because of a shared regional heritage. For the first time as a pro football player, I felt comfortable, and it was on one of the historically worst teams in football.

Business Calls

I played my first game for the Saints in week seven. The team had managed to scrape together a record of two wins and four losses, and was getting set to play against the Washington Redskins at Tulane Stadium.

I sat in the locker room, getting ready to play in black and gold for the first time. It was a bit humbling to realize where I was sitting. I was three years into the league and I had not become the all-star starter that I had dreamed of being at the beginning of my journey. I realized that soon I would be walking down the tunnel in a river of fifty other players dressed just like me, and nobody would even care to point me out in the crowd. It was humbling. It maybe even would have bothered me a year prior, but since then, I had grown to acquire a new set of goals—goals that were about more than football, about more than myself. My new goals included being a good husband and father, being able to provide financially for my family, being a man of good character, and being the best that I could be in every field of life.

There was nothing spectacular about my performance in the game. I gained 20 yards rushing and 30 yards receiving as the team went on to get their third win. But after the game, I was given the game ball for my efforts. That was one of the most meaningful moments in my professional football career.

It was after that game, though, that the real work began. As soon as the game ended, I headed back down that same tunnel that connected the field with the locker room. I was the first one in the shower and I was the first one getting dressed. One of my teammates asked me, "Joe, what's your hurry? We just finished a game."

I looked in the mirror while I struggled to fix the tie around my neck. In between tugs, I managed to eke out, "Can't stay long . . . Got a plane to catch." In the mirror, I saw Archie Manning with a swarm of local reporters huddled around his locker. There were people shouting his name and prodding him with microphones, I figured he could barely breathe. Looking back, I guess it was a blessing that I hadn't had a lot of fanfare surrounding my name. If I had, I would have had to stick around and shoot the bull just like him.

I fled the locker like a phantom, without even breathing another word to any of my teammates. My wife met me outside the stadium with our car. I jumped in, told her about the game, and then she hit the gas and peeled off toward the highway.

As we sped to New Orleans International Airport, the words echoed in my mind. Why are you in such a hurry? For everyone else in that locker room, the question made sense. That was their work. They had a whole day and a half to relax and recover, but for me it was a different story.

My wife dropped me off at the terminal as the sun was resting low in the western sky. I only had a few minutes to make my flight for Atlanta.

That's right, I was heading for Atlanta. While all others in the

NFL would be kicking back in their recliners tonight, icing their muscles and watching TV, I would be flipping pancakes at IHOP.

I continued this every single week. I would get done with the game, shower up, then head straight for the airport. I would work an overnight shift at one of my restaurants, and then catch a flight back to New Orleans Monday afternoon. If everything went on schedule, I would be back in time to get some sleep before practice on Tuesday morning.

My coach thought it was weird. On the second week, he asked me, "Joe, what are you up to that you need to be out here in such a hurry?"

When I explained my predicament, he just rattled off on the same "your job is football" lecture that I heard endlessly from Rankin Smith. Still, he thought it was more funny that disruptive. He couldn't figure out why I would be so devoted, "to a restaurant" he would say. My teammates felt the same way. After a few weeks, they all got in the habit of saying "see ya, Joe!" right as the game ended, knowing it was the last they would see of me. Even after away games, when we would fly back to New Orleans during the late hours of the night, I would watch my teammates tread away to their cars while I stayed in the terminal, waiting to transfer to my flight to Atlanta.

Skipping town week after week was tiresome. It took a toll on me physically, mentally and emotionally, but I knew that the outcome was more important than the process. My mom and dad raised me to be the best I could be, so I never wanted to let them down by settling for less. Was playing football adequate? Yes. Did it support my family? Yes. But I knew I could do more, so I did. At the same time, I felt it was good for my restaurants. They seemed to be fueled by my appearances. I know that if I had been flipping burgers for a professional football player as a kid, I would have thought it was pretty cool, but if that professional football player actually came in and talked to me and worked hand-in-hand with me, I would have been thrilled! I really just wanted to let them know that I cared.

Because of my devotion, I saw the benefits of being a hard-working man in the business world. I had learned early, much to the credit of Rankin Smith and his colleagues at Life of Georgia. I proved that even small businesses could be more profitable than a football contract—especially in those days. Before the 1973 season ended, I was making more as a restaurant owner than I was as a football player—and I was only working there one day as opposed to six. I figured that wasn't too bad of a gig.

A Whole New World

The Saints and I ended the season with a 5-9 record. We missed the playoffs, but it was still the best record in the team's short history. Best of all, I was enjoying the team I was playing for. Still, during the offseason, I got a call that turned my career upside down.

The call was from the Birmingham Americans. The who? You might ask. I don't blame you. If you were born in the 1970s or later, you've probably never heard of them, and if you were born before then, well, there's still a fair chance you've never heard of them either. They were from the World Football League—a league that was attempting to challenge the NFL and its monopoly in the same way the AFL had a few years earlier—and they were scouting players such as myself to jump over to their side.

But I was skeptical, to say the least. Not only was I very comfortable with my position on the Saints; I couldn't think of any way an upstart league could offer me anything better. Well, they proved me wrong. The starting salary they offered me was worth more than my contract in the NFL, and as a signing bonus, they were prepared to offer me a free Mercedes convertible. When the team owner, Mr. William "Bill" Putnam told me about the offer, I thought he was playing a prank, but when he told me all the other big names that were considering the jump—Charley Haraway, former NFL Rookie of the year Paul Robinson, Alfred Jenkins, Dennis Homan, John Matlock and others—I thought for the first time, this must be for real.

The Saints became angry when they found out that I was in talks with Birmingham. Naturally, they wanted their players focused on their own team, so anything I did with a different team was considered a distraction. In training camp of the following year, I pulled my thigh muscle and had to sit out for a few days. When I returned to practice on Sunday, I was informed that I had been released from the team. That very afternoon, I got Mr. Putnam on the phone, and we negotiated a contract with Birmingham.

By now, you may be screaming at these pages, saying, "Joe, what were you thinking?! You had it made and you decided to risk it all!" Well, you certainly may have a point there. At that time in my life, I was just beginning to work out the blueprints of my "rules on economics" which I share later in this book. I had established ground rules such as "Be a networker" and "Take advantage of every opportunity", but I had little to say on risk-taking. Thus far in my life, I had been rewarded in most every risk I had taken, and I didn't see any risk in signing a lucrative contract. In my eyes, the owners and the operators were the ones that would need to worry.

Nonetheless, as the first season unfolded, there were painful signs of mismanagement everywhere. Some teams could not pay for their own transportation or lodging. Some teams could not even afford laundry or medical equipment, and had to cancel practices. Other teams failed to pay their players altogether—giving checks that bounced, which destroyed the credibility of the league. Notoriously, a few teams either changed location or folded completely midway through the season. From the start, the league was a mess, and the players were rightfully nervous.

I kept my head on by continuing to operate my restaurants. Although I was now living in Birmingham, I kept my tradition of flying back to Atlanta on a weekly basis, just as I had during my time with the Saints. While my restaurants continued to make money, I could see from the outside how risky my venture into WFL really was. Players all around me were falling into a financial hole, and they had no means to pull themselves out. I realized that my businesses were the only things keeping me from the same destructive fate, so I sat down and added two rules to my list: "Be a risk-taker" and "Avoid taking too many risks". I decided that in my life I would need to take risks to achieve success, but the risks should never be more than I am prepared to lose. With my WFL contract, I may not have exactly been prepared to lose, but I surely had enough to back it up. I consider myself blessed, and very lucky.

Despite all the league's failures, it was still competitive. The talent between teams was very evenly matched, which made for close scores and exciting games. The Birmingham Americans were one of the only teams that stayed afloat throughout the entire season, which was astounding, as the schedule consisted of 20 regular season games, as opposed to the NFL's then 14-game season. The team owner Bill Putnam, was also the owner of the NHL's Philadelphia Flyers, and had a lot of money from his other business endeavors and investments, so he was able to follow through on all of the player contracts.

Personally, I was able to start for the Americans at running back, which allowed me to perform at a much higher level than I had in the NFL. I was one of the leading rushers in the league, and helped the Americans reach the first—and only—World Bowl championship game.

By that time, the fanfare had dwindled to almost nothing, as the once-promising league was lost in the shadows of the NFL. We still played the championship, which was against the Florida Blazers, but even that game was saturated with the same kind of follies that had defined the league all throughout the season. The referees missed on several key calls that would have changed the game. Embarrassing fights broke out between the players and coaches. At halftime, the league awarded the season MVP award, which was split between three players. The prize was a literal stack of cash on a table (as the league was unable to write a trustworthy check) and it was divided among the three players equally.

In the game, I ran for 60 yards, recorded 1 touchdown, and was named Most Valuable Player, helping my team to a 22-21 victory. But the real spectacle of the game happened after the final whistle blew. As soon as we got back to the locker room, the league informed us that the bank was seizing all of the team's property. They forced us then and there to shed our uniforms and turn them over for seizure. We were forced to celebrate our championship victory half-naked with no gear or equipment.

The end of the game signaled, for all intents and purposes, the painful end to a laughing-stock of a league. We would play the following year, as the Birmingham Vulcans, but the league folded eight games into the season and we were named champions only by record.

The WFL, which was mocked by the media under the name "Wiffle", was a failure of a league. Many players, coaches and executives lost their jobs and their investments simply because of a poorly-structured business plan. But by the Lord's blessing, I was able to survive. Even after the league folded, I still had my other career to fall back on. This is why I have been stressing the importance of seeking success in many fields. You never know what lies ahead in a risk-laden world, but if you have a plan in place for the worst possible outcome, you really can't fail.

10 Ten

MAKING A HISTORICAL IMPACT

Leaving the Second Field

At the end of the 1975 season, I decided not to return to the NFL. My restaurants were overwhelmingly more profitable by then, so it didn't make sense to stage a comeback.

Though it was strange to be exiting football after playing the game all my life, I was not at all devastated by the transition. I thought back to my time in the hospital, when I was struggling to regain my walk, and the doctors told me I would never run again. When I told them I had a five-year plan they laughed in my face, but there I was, having played for five years, just like had I said. The Lord had provided me with that much time, and I was proud of myself for taking full advantage of His blessing. Just making it that far in my career felt to me like I had obliterated the odds, and demolished the low expectations.

But the most comforting part of all was the knowledge that I had a new career to fall back on. I cannot stress enough how much of a blessing this was to me and my family. Without it—without the days waiting patiently outside Mr. Smith's office, without the help of people like Mr. Patrick H. Robinson, without the upbringing of my father—I would have had nothing. I would have been stranded in the cold, cruel world. Instead, at the age of 26, I had a plan for my life that would last forever, and I was ready to retire from the temporary career of football.

If anything, this is the reason I want you to hear my story. Even if you are a student still going to school, I believe that you are never too young to start looking toward your long-term goals. You are never too young to accomplish something great. Don't let anyone—even the big guys—stand in your way if you know what you're doing is right. If you have something blocking your path, turn it into a stepping stone and push forward.

Now I was fully transitioned into my life as a restaurant owner and operator. Along the way, I continued to acquire more franchises, but my tenure in the food industry would only last for a few more years. It all started when I acquired a Jilly's Restaurant (The place for ribs!) at a location in downtown Atlanta at 89 Luckie Street, which had been the previous address of the old Atlanta Playboy club. When Playboy moved out, we were left to excavate the property and convert it into a family restaurant.

I thought it was funny, and so did a number of other people. Shortly after moving in, I got a call from my stock broker, who summarized the idea perfectly, "So let me get this straight. Your name is Joe Profit, you're a successful businessman, and you run your business at 89 Luckie Street . . . at the site of the old Playboy club?"

I laughed, "You got that right."

"Joe," he said, "That sounds all too perfect. I'll bet you're covering up a super hero identity, too."

I laughed and told him no. There was no super-human strength involved in getting me to where I was. There was only hard work and determination. I kept my corporate office in a central location at the Equitable

Building, also in downtown Atlanta, so that I could keep an eye on all of my restaurants at once. One day, when I arrived at the building, I was in a hurry and tried to catch the elevator. There was only one man inside, and as the doors were closing, he saw me coming and put his hand in the way.

"Thanks," I said.

"Not a problem." He studied me for a moment, and then said, "Do I know you from somewhere?"

"Well, that depends." I said, "I used to play football for the Falcons a few years back."

"Yeah, that's right! You played running back, didn't you?" He held out his hand, "My name is Matthew H. Patton, Attorney."

"Joe Profit," I said, and shook his hand.

After making small talk, we found out that we not only worked in the same building together, but we lived in the same neighborhood only three blocks apart.

I said, "Matthew, you've got to be kidding me. Of all the places to live in a city as big as Atlanta, it must be fate that we met on this elevator."

He laughed, "So Joe, if you don't mind me asking . . . you're out of football, what do you do for your work nowadays?"

"Now I operate a string of restaurants. Mainly Jilly's, Burger King and—Gourmet Pizza "

He cut me off, "You're kidding, Joe! That's what I do too! I work at a law firm, but I run a Burger King on the side!" The elevator nearly burst apart right there. We had only just met, but we still had three huge things in common. "Well, I guess it must be fate. Joe, we gotta go out for lunch sometime and talk business."

I shook his hand and said, "Sure thing. How about today?"

We met up on that same elevator later that day and went out to a nearby restaurant (at our own discretion, we decided against Burger King). During our conversation, as I had the tendency to do, I asked him about his work. I said, "So you're a lawyer and you run a restaurant. What kind of work does that involve?"

He said, "Well, to tell you the truth, that's only a small part of what I do. These days, I'm working more in the political world than anything else." I was intrigued. Since being involved at Northeast with the Young Republicans, I had always brought an interest in politics with me wherever I went, but I had never delved too deeply into the world of politics itself. Matthew went on to tell me how he was the Chairman of the Republican Party of Georgia, and he had been campaigning for Ronald Reagan for the past year. When I told him that I was a conservative too, he almost choked on his food. He had a hard time believing there were any conservative black men in the entire country. Immediately, he said, "I've got to introduce you to Ted Stivers."

What had been a chance encounter earlier that morning was quickly morphing into one of the more pivotal points of my life? Matthew H. Patton took me to the Republican headquarters later that day and introduced me to Ted Stivers, the co-chairman of the party.

"Joe here is a Republican," Matthew said, "and he's looking to help with the Reagan campaign."

Both of us, Ted and I, looked at him in bewilderment. I had only said that I was a conservative, and I never mentioned anything about campaigning. Ted was busy comprehending the big, black conservative that had just entered his office.

It was all happening so fast for me. It was only a few days later when I received a phone call from Ted. He told me that he had been talking with Matthew, and they asked me to be chairman of Blacks for Reagan. By that time, I had already been a supporter of Governor Reagan. I felt personally that his ideologies for job creation were exactly what the country needed (I always felt a person would rather have a job than food stamps or welfare), and that the opposition Jimmy Carter's ideologies, if continued, would do well only to demolish the economy. Carter, being a Georgia native, already had a large majority of the state's vote, and even more of a majority of the black vote, but I realized that with my position I could help make a dent in the statistics, if anything. I accepted the offer.

Politics in those days were a little bit different than they are now. There was certainly a lot of tension left over in the wake of the Vietnam War, but for the most part, Republicans and Democrats worked together. Nowadays, they stay segregated, and they view any act of compromise as a sign of weakness.

To give you an impression of my attitude, I'll tell you at first that I was not strictly a Republican. I was conservative, yes, but I did not affiliate only with that one party. Prior to working with the Reagan campaign, I joined numerous other campaigns around the country in favor of policies that which I thought were beneficial for specific communitites.

When John Conyers, a Democrat from Detroit, was running for election to Congress, I invited him down to 103 West, a restaurant in

Atlanta, where we held a fundraiser for his campaign. When the day was done, we had raised over $13,000. He came up to me after the event, amazed, and said, "That was the first time I have ever held a fundraiser outside of Michigan, and wouldn't you know it, it was all done by a black Republican from Georgia. Joe, you just might go far in this world."

A few weeks into my duties on the Reagan campaign, I got a call from Lyn Nofziger, Governor Reagan's advisor and press secretary. He told me that Reagan was looking to get more Democrats to back his campaign, which meant gaining more of the black vote. One of the first surprise backers of Reagan was Congresswoman and civil rights activist Shirley Chisholm—the first black woman ever elected to Congress. Despite being a Democrat from New York, Chisholm joined the campaign quietly after rejecting President Carter's ideologies. However, after news broke nationally, she came under fire from many of her fellow Democrats, and she was all but forced to reconsider her options.

Ted and Lyn called me into the office one night to discuss our options. When I got there, the first thing out of Ted's mouth was, "Joe, I won't beat around the bush. We need a prominent black Democrat to endorse Reagan.

Now tell us; what can you do?"

I said what about two? Ted fell silent, and then replied, "This is serious Joe! The Governor is in trouble we need someone now. I brought up the names Dr. Ralph David Abernathy and Reverend Hosea Williams. When I mentioned their names, Ted's eyes went wide, "David Abernathy and Hosea Williams? You're talking about the right-hand men of Dr. Martin Luther King Jr.?"

I explained to them how I knew the two reverends. I had worked on some business deals with Dr. Abernathy in the past, and I had collaborated with Reverend Williams on several business opportunities as well. I was on more than just speaking terms with both of them, and they both lived and worked in the Atlanta community.

Ted leaned forward in his chair with his elbows on the table. "Joe," he said, "don't waste our time here. There's no way you can get those guys on our side."

But I still had confidence. I knew that the reverends each spoke with firm, established voices, but behind those voices were men that were open to reason. I told them, "Just give me a few minutes."

I stepped into the next room, picked up the phone and called David Abernathy. When I told him what I wanted, the phone in my hand nearly shorted out. He said, "Joe, why are you wasting my time? You know that black people are going to stick with Carter. He's a Democrat."

I said, "Yes sir, I know that. And I know that the black population will stick with Carter . . . unless they see that other black people are backing Reagan."

I couldn't see because I was on the phone, but I could practically hear the reverend shaking his head on the other end. He thought for a moment, and then said, "Well, I can't put my faith in Reagan, but on the other hand I can't put my faith in Carter at all. I'd rather vote a rock into office than him again." He took another long, drawn out pause. I didn't want to say anything, because I could tell that the conversation was going in the right direction and I didn't want to do anything to screw that up. Finally, he said, "Joe, here's what I'll do. I'll talk to Hosea and see what the man has to say. If we work something out, we work something out, but you can't expect me to just hop the line after one phone call."

"I understand. I appreciate your time, Reverend."

Then he added, "Joe, a lot of people think we had the answer with Carter, but he wasn't the answer, and he isn't the answer. Now, do you really believe that Ronald Reagan is the answer?"

I said, "Well, there's only one way to find out."

I got off the phone and walked back into the office. The rest of the gang was silent. They could clearly overhear my conversation, and they were stunned that I wasn't blowing any smoke when it came to dealing with the reverends. I sat back down, and Matthew said, "Well done, Joe."

Dr. Abernathy called me back the next day. He said they had talked it over, and agreed that I had a point—that they would do good to lure votes away from President Carter, yet they were hesitant about giving Reagan an actual endorsement. They still did not believe they had seen enough out of him to be sure of his commitment to the people. Obviously, as activists for civil rights, they did not want to risk endorsing someone who would demolish the integrity of the recovering African-American and minority communities.

I told them again that I understood. So far, they had given me the best that I could have asked for.

"Well," I said, "I appreciate your consideration. The last thing I will say is that I believe Ronald Reagan will be fair and equitable, and I know that he will be a strong leader."

"I'm glad you feel so strongly, Joe. I really am. And I hope you're right, too. I guess only time will tell."

"Thank you, Reverend."

" We'll keep in touch. If there's anything else I can do for you in the meantime, just let me know."

But I wasn't ready to hang up just yet. Again, I remembered one of my most trusted principles; never close a door when you don't have to. I said, "Well, there is one last thing. My co-chairs and I are hosting a fundraiser dinner event for the Reagan campaign tonight. I understand your reluctance to fully endorse him, but if you would like to come anyway . . . as a guest . . . you are certainly welcome."

"As a guest?"

I smiled, "The door will be open, and there will be good food and drinks! That's all I'm saying at this time. God bless, Reverend."

The Reverend said, "Hold on Joe, if we come to your fundraiser tonight that means that we are in…"

At the fundraiser that night, things were going very well. We had rented a banquet/reception space a top of the Equatiable Building in downtown Atlanta, and we featured several speakers on behalf of Reagan. None, of course, were as noteworthy as the men that I had hoped to see, but the two reverends were nowhere to be found. I delivered a speech near the closing of the event in which I encouraged the black population to consider Reagan—a potential advocate of the black community. I think my presence was enough to make a statement, at least to the white people who were continually impressed to see a black man at the podium, but the number of black guests was miniscule. I felt alone up on that podium, like I really was one of few black leaders in the Country supporting Reagan. Without the endorsement of a leading black Democrat of national status, it was hard for people to believe my words.

By the time I finished my speech, it was almost nine in the evening; Club employees were getting ready to close the doors, and the audience was weaning out. Ted walked over to me and said, "Oh, Joe, everything's going just fine, but I don't believe just fine is good enough." Georgia is a Carter state. We really could have used Dr. Abernathy and Hosea Williams."

I felt a bit slighted at his remark. I had done the best I could, but there was still a feeling of responsibility, that I hadn't achieved what I had set out to do. "I'm sorry," I said.

"No. Don't you feel sorry? You've been the biggest help of anyone. We're all so thankful that you" He stopped mid-sentence.

"What's wrong?" I said. I looked at the door, and to my surprise, I saw Dr. Ralph David Abernathy and Hosea Williams entering the room. I knew at that moment, that they were going to endorse Governor Reagan for President.

His eyes went wide. I traced them over to the same door, where Dr. David Ralph Abernathy and Hosea Williams, both in full suits, had just entered my Ronald Reagan campaign fundraiser. I patted Ted on the shoulder and said, "I'll be right back."

I walked over to the Dr. Abernathy and Reverend Williams and shook their hands. "Welcome, gentlemen." I said. Those were the only words I could eke out of my mouth, which was clenched tightly in a silly grin. By then the entire crowd had their heads turned in our direction, and the room was void of sound. It was clear from their faces that the reverends had not expected to make this much of an entrance, but I suppose that two of the nation's best known black Democrats would appear conspicuous in an assembly of whites, at a Republican fundraiser for Ronald Reagan.

"I was told there would be a meal waiting for me," said Dr. Abernathy. His face was stoic.

"Yes, sir. We'll bring out a meal for both of you." Everyone else had already finished eating, and the caterers had collected all of the dishes, but I was going to make sure those men got a meal even if I had to go out and hunt the game myself. I turned toward the kitchen, but Reverend Abernathy grabbed my arm and turned me back.

"Son, go sit down. You've worked hard enough already."

The two of them strode across the room, captivating the attention of the entire room as though they owned the place. I took a seat in back, and Ted came to sit next to me.

"What did they say?!" he asked in an ecstatic whisper.

"Nothing. They said they wanted a meal. Then they walked to the stage."

I waited as Dr. Abernathy cleared his throat. My hands were twitching nervously. He certainly was taking his time. Finally he said, "Ladies and gentlemen. Thank you for coming to our banquet tonight. It's wonderful to see that so many people have come together in support of the next President of the United States."

I let out a sigh and smiled. All I could think was Thank God.

Dr. Abernathy and Reverend Williams announced their endorsement of Reagan formally to the public in Kansas City early the next day. After the announcement was made Reagan was asked quoted as saying "I didn't think such a thing could happen." Before leaving Atlanta, they had asked me to come with and join them at the big public announcement, but I told them that my work was done—that it was all about them now and a new sprite of bipartisanship.

When the news hit the media, it felt like the sky was falling. Black voters were swept off their heels at the thought of their activist leaders taking what they thought to be the other side. Voters and media analysts could see no reason for the endorsement, noting that they and their friend, Dr. King, had historically refused to endorse any candidate.

All while the media speculated, I stayed back in the shadows and let the men do their work. Apart from the congratulations I received from my Republican friends, I had already felt a strong sense of inner accomplishment. I felt that I had used my resources to help change the world on a much larger scale than I could have done alone. The idea that I had made a difference meant so much to me. I consider this one of the biggest achievements of my life: the endorsement of Ronald Regan for President of the United States by two of the most respected Civil Rights leaders of the Day, Dr. Ralph David Abernathy and Reverend Hosea Williams.

Win One for the GOP

Governor Reagan, of course, went on to win the election by a landslide, and though Carter took all of Georgia (as expected), I knew that I had made a difference. Reverends Abernathy and Williams went all across the South during their campaign, and made a difference in an area much larger than Georgia alone.

Nowadays, I don't even know if President Reagan would have even gotten a nomination, based on the way the political world has changed. We've seen an economic recession in which a lot of fingers got pointed and a lot of nothing got accomplished. I think the finger pointing needs to stop and we need to return to our ways of inter-party cooperation. We need to humble ourselves and realize that we may not have all the answers. We need to listen to one another and be open to changing our minds. The two reverends made an endorsement after a change of heart, and in the end they were praised for their bold move. I think we need to have the same mentality today. That way, we can learn to let down our fingers and work toward making a real difference.

Working with The Greatest

Early in the 1980s, Atlanta gained national attention as the location of many child abductions and murders over the span of two years. It was a troubling time in the city. Because of the tragedy, the people began to lose faith in their police force, and the city felt unsafe as a whole. As a result, there was a lot of finger pointing, and those fingers eventually became clustered in groups divided by race. The white community widely believed that a black man was responsible, while the black community insisted that the modern Ku Klux Klan was to blame. Because of this, the city became divided, and it only led to more hatred.

Up to that time, my businesses were doing very well, but the tragedy took a toll on almost every thriving business in the city. It was hard to be profitable, and it was hard to be optimistic. But instead of accepting the situation, I decided that I wanted to help—if nothing else, to ease the tension between the two sides, so that we could focus our time and money on bringing a stop to the murders.

I called in several favors from close friends in order to start fundraisers to bring the criminal or criminals to justice. The fundraisers were moderately successful, but not as much as I had hoped. I thought about ways to draw more attention to the matter, and remembered that I had been introduced to Muhammad Ali by a mutual friend several years earlier while I was still in football. Ali was and still is a strong activist for civil rights, and he had no doubt taken an interest in the nationally-broadcasted story, so I got on the phone and invited him to attend the fundraiser, and to stay at my home during his visit.

He was overwhelmingly supportive. He flew out to Atlanta shortly after and stayed at my house for the weekend. During his speech at the fundraiser, he emphasized the need for our society to come together as one. He urged the people of Atlanta not to turn away from each other, but to bond together and strengthen each other in this time of need. Lastly, he announced that he would donate nearly half a million dollars to the cause.

The donation made an overwhelming impact on the city. Through the tragic nature of the events, a community was finally able to come together and accept that, black or white, we were all in it together.

On the Road

Later in the year, I held a fundraiser for John Tower, a Republican from Texas who was running for re-election to the Senate. I flew out to Washington D.C. to deliver a speech about conservatism and the black community. The speech was similar to the one I delivered in Atlanta, but it was on a bigger stage, and it lasted over an hour.

When I got down from the podium, I was approached by a man

about my age. "Joe Profit," he said as he shook my hand, "My name is Joe Reeder."

"Pleasure to meet you, Mr. Reeder."

"And you as well. It was a blessing hearing you speak today, Mr. Profit. When I saw you take the podium, I thought, 'Wow! What is a black man from Georgia doing at an event for a white man from Texas? To tell you the truth, I have never seen any black person who was a true conservative before."

I smiled, "Well, we're around. You just have to go far enough south."

He reciprocated the smile. Later down the line, Joe would become the United States Under Secretary of the Army, but at the time of the fundraiser, he was a recent graduate of law school, and had just started working as a lawyer for Patton Boggs in Washington.

"Is there something I can help you with?" I said.

"Well, not exactly, but I was hoping that I could be of help to you." He handed me a business card. "I may be young in the business, Mr. Profit, but one thing I do know is that minorities are discriminated against in the court. If you're ever in any legal trouble, you just give me a call."

I thanked him, even though I did not see his point at the time. My businesses were running great, and I couldn't imagine what kind of legal trouble he was talking about. Out of formality I decided to keep his card, and we parted company. Little did I know that he would eventually come back play a huge role in my life.

Later while attending the same event, I was introduced to Alan Rand with the Rand Corporation. As Joe Reeder had expressed, he was also impressed that I had even made an appearance at such an event. He was moved by my speech, and asked me to join him for lunch.

While we were eating, he picked my brain dry. He wanted to know all about my background, and my upbringing. I told him about growing up in Lake Providence, about working in the field with my family and playing football for my school. Then I told him about my work as an entrepreneur in the restaurant business. He seemed truly fascinated by everything I had been through.

Then I asked him about himself, and about the type work he did. I learned he was doing telecommunications work for the government, supplying equipment for the military.

"That's why I was so interested in hearing your story, Mr. Profit. See, I've been searching all around the country for a strong conservative minority that could help with my work."

"Why do you need me?" I said.

"Well, for starters, you're a true conservative. I heard your speech, and only a true conservative could so strongly address an audience with conviction like you did. I felt the power coming through your words."

"And why do you need a minority?"

"Well, plain and simple. We need someone to give us insight from another viewpoint. Imagine a bunch of white guys trying to appeal to America at large—well, I guess that's how the government is right now, but that's beside the point. We're trying to get input from a variety of sources, and I think you could help us do that."

"But Mr. Rand, with all due respect, I've never delved outside of the restaurant business. If I were to work in telecommunications, I would have no idea what I'm doing."

He laughed, "That's not a problem at all. Neither do any of us! All we're looking for is a businessman, and you fit that credential perfectly."

I returned home and thought it over. In all honesty, I had built a comfortable nest in my restaurant business, and I wasn't looking for anything to get in the way. But after considering it further, I realized that it would be a good thing to add to my repertoire. Who knows, I thought, maybe I would be able to help people, too. I contacted Mr. Rand a few days later and agreed that I would join the project.

When we finished working the project, he told me I had done a fantastic job, far better than he had expected. He said, "You know, Joe, you're really good at working in communications. You should really stay in the business."

I learned from the project that I really did enjoy working in the communications industry. It was not only a profitable business, but I loved the fact that its goal was to bring us closer together as humans. I remember the nights at Northeast when I would sit in my room, isolated from everyone else on campus because of their hatred of me. I craved the support of my home community, and even though they were only across town, they might as well have been on a different planet. I would have given just about anything to be able to call home to my parents for support.

Riding the emotional wave from my success with Mr. Rand, I decided to follow through on his advice; I was going to start my own communications company. I went back to 89 Luckie Street to map it all out—the beginnings of what would become my first real company,

Communications International, Incorporated.

There was no describing the pride that I had felt in myself after I started that company. I thought first of my family, who had been supportive in not only encouraging me, but raising me to believe that I could achieve anything I wanted. I thought of my coach and hero, Mr. Robinson, who had first inspired me to be more than another face in the crowd. I thought of my wife and children (by this time, we had Joseph Jr. and our newest daughter, Cara), who had stayed strong despite me being away from home on so many nights. I realized then that I wasn't the only one who had made it happen. All along, I had depended on others to build me up. The support was so great, it seemed like everyone else had started the job for me, and all I had to do was to bring it to completion.

Though it was a little company at first (we only had a handful of employees, and continued to work out of the basement of my Jilly's), Communications International was a very determined little company. In that first year, we were constantly submitting bids for work. The Atlanta community was such a large and modernized city that there was a high demand for communications providers, but with that high demand, there were about a million and one other companies just like us clawing for a job. So we decided to branch out of the metropolitan area.

We started submitting bids all over the south—South Carolina, Mississippi, Alabama, and even Louisiana. Then one day, while we were doing little more than twiddling our thumbs, I got a phone call. It was from the mayor's office. But not the mayor of Atlanta, mind you. It was the mayor of Tuskegee, Alabama. The little town of less than ten thousand people apparently needed new telephones and wiring in their city hall, and they had received ours as the only bid for the job. I hung up the phone, smiled and said to the rest, "We're going to Alabama."

We were bouncing off the walls, and the ceiling just about blew off at 89 Luckie Street. The next day, we set out for Tuskegee as a brand new, energized team.

Business began booming soon after that. We did such a good job in Tuskegee that we were able to start marketing our brand in Atlanta with a positive reference. Let this be a lesson that even the smallest jobs can do wonders for promoting your brand. Don't ever count them out.

With Tuskegee as a reference, we were able to land more jobs in markets closer to home, and eventually, our business burgeoned. Soon it became apparent that we were beginning to outgrow the basement of 89 Luckie Street.

After only six months in the business, I got back into contact with Alan Rand. He was pleased to see how far I had come in such a short time, but asserted that he knew I was capable. He then informed me that the United States Department of Defense was looking for submissions for a new project, similar to the one that he and I had collaborated on less than a year earlier. Well, that was all it took for me to get my people on board for a submission, and with his help, the little company from Georgia was able to get a job with the U.S. government.

Making of a National Holiday

In late October, 1983, I got another call from Lyn Nofziger, who was an advisor to the President. He informed me that the political main stream media had turned its attention to the congressional debate over Martin Luther King, Jr. Day. The Congress had overwhelmingly voted in favor of creating the national holiday, but there were still some who were reluctant to sign. One of those people was President Reagan.

"It's looking like he's not going to sign it into law," Lyn said, "What do you think?"

"Well, doesn't he have to sign it if Congress votes on it?" I asked.

"Not necessarily, but even so, he's been trying to convince Congress to vote against the bill."

"Why is that?"

Lynn paused to think for a moment, and then he said, "It's the economy. He feels another national holiday would only do damage to the country." I could see the reasoning behind it. If the country stopped working for a day, we would lose money, and money was everything in a globalized economy. But personally, I was in favor of the law, and if you've read this far in my book, it should be easy to see why. All my life I had grown up as a second-class citizen. The notion of a black man being honored by the nation would have been wishful thinking back then, but now it had the chance to become a reality. Lynn continued, "Joe, you and I both know Reagan respects African-Americans. But he's being pressured by the party to keep the economy in mind. It's not an issue of race to him."

"Well," I said, "it may not be an issue of race to him, but it is to the people. So far, Reagan has done a great job of running the country. But sometimes doing the right thing is better than doing the conservative thing or doing the profitable thing. Sometimes doing the right thing is best for the country. I think if he wants to do the right thing, he'd better get his pen out and sign the paper."

"I guess I can't argue with that," he said. "I'll get President Reagan on the line and see what we can make happen."

I hung up the phone and waited. In less than half an hour, Lyn called me back.

"Hello?" I said.

"Joe, its Lyn. Just calling to say we got him."

"Wait, what?"

"We got him to sign. He's going to sign the bill once it passes through congress."

"But—but that was only thirty minutes, at most! How did you guys convince him in that short of time?"

"Well, I told the President exactly what you told me. I don't know how it happened. We were able to reach his heart, I guess."

I felt a sense of warmth flow through my body. The president listened? I thought. He listened to the African American people? I wasn't surprised at all that he had—I was just shocked that it took him so little time to change his mind.

On November 2, President Reagan held a ceremony for the signing of the law. The President was still very reluctant about the law, even on the day of the signing, and long afterward as well, but he did agree that it was good for the hearts of the American people. In attendance to oversee the ceremony was Coretta Scott King, Dr. King's widow. She stood next to the President as thousands watched him sign the paper. The presence of both of them on the stage at the same time was a strong statement. It signaled that unity and integration were on the rise in America. We had come a long way, and we were progressing toward a more equal nation.

I personally treasure the fact that we, the Republicans of Georgia, were able to help push the President in what we felt was the right direction. After his tenure in office ended in 1989, the signing of Martin Luther King, Jr. Day into law came to be regarded as one of the major highlights of Reagan's Presidency. It was a great day for the African-American community, and it was a great day for America as a whole. The fact that I was able to help bring it to fruition is one of my most cherished accomplishments.

11 Eleven

ROADBLOCKS TO STEPPING STONES

Conquering a Roadblock with Teamwork

All while I worked in the political world, Communications International continued to grow. Although we originally started in the basement of my restaurant, we were now operating out of several offices across the South. In 1986, we won a Department of Defense contract to work with the United States government at Military Ocean Terminal Sunny Point (MOTSU), the largest military terminal in the world. MOTSU needed a complete reconstruction of their phone system, including cabling for their outside lines, both buried and aerial, with fiber optics.

In the days preceding the project, the Army sent our entire team the special clearance papers and identification that we needed to enter the base, and they declared secret status to our entire operation. Then, as a team, we traveled to the base in Wilmington, North Carolina. But once we reached the base at Sunny Point, we were stopped by an Army official and told that we could not enter. I explained that we had special clearance, and that we had all the papers we needed, but the man would not let us through. Apparently, Bobby DeWitt, the man in charge, asserted that we should not be granted access.

When we returned to our hotel that night, I got on the phone with the men in Washington, D.C. and explained what had happened. They assured me, "Joe, just show up tomorrow and it will all be taken care of."

The next day, however, we were still not granted access. I asked to see Bobby DeWitt in person, but in order to speak with him, he had to walk to the edge of the base and speak with me through the barrier.

"Mr. DeWitt," I said, "Your men aren't letting us in. We have a contract with the Army, and we have all the papers we need. We should be able to come in."

But Bobby DeWitt was as cold as ice. He said, "I don't care what the Army says. You boys aren't touching our phone lines!" I didn't like how he referred to us as boys. We were there in our professional uniforms, and we were acting like professional men should. None of it made sense to me.

Finally, I got Washington on the line again, and they convinced Bobby to let us on the base. A few days later, we learned the reason he didn't want us there; we were a minority company, and he "didn't want the blacks handling the Army's phone systems." It was a shock that someone so powerful could make such a statement and get away with it at that time in our country's history.

But one thing I learned from my dad is that you have to be persistent. Although some people are mean-spirited, it doesn't mean you have to be as well. Thus, we got to work. We completed the task as planned, and we did it better than expected. Instead of installing new cabling just on the outside of the plant, we installed it on the inside as well, stringing together a network of over one thousand phone lines. But Bobby DeWitt did not address any member of our team, even once, until the end of the project. To him, it was like we weren't even there. When we finished, he only said one thing, "Well, you can all go home now."

We still didn't understand. Normally they had scheduled a small ceremony announcing the signing over, or 'cutting over,' of the deal, which was meant to signify that, the project had been completed. It also was the point at which we were to be paid. But Bobby DeWitt said that he wouldn't sign.

Well, you can imagine our frustration. By this time we were about ready as a team to knock Mr. DeWitt upside the head. But what was even more infuriating was that people had come from all around the country for the ceremony. When he refused to sign, it created a stir among everyone there.

Finally, our representative from CII was so fed up that he took me to Mr. DeWitt's office, where he locked the door and forced him to sign. And I mean that literally. He grabbed Mr. DeWitt by the hand, crammed a pen between his fist and scraped his signature across the paper. Mr. DeWitt screamed in protest, but the deed was done.

In the ensuing weeks, we waited for the check to come in the mail, but it never came. Again, we did not understand any of it. We had completed the task, and completed it well. We had done everything that had been asked of us. The fact that we were a minority company did not affect the project or the result. Why, then, would he refuse to pay us?

It was at that time that I had my secretary look up the name of the attorney I had met in Washington years earlier. His name was Joe Reeder, and he was still working for Patton Boggs. I got on the phone with Joe, and he took little time convincing me to take action against the Army. This was a big statement for him, as he was a graduate of United States Military Academy, and would later serve as the Under Secretary of the Army under President Clinton. With his advice, I took action against Mr. DeWitt.

The atmosphere in the courtroom during the trial could only be described as shock and awe. It seemed that nobody in the entire room believed Bobby DeWitt had any right to refuse our payment. I'll bet he had a hard time even convincing himself. But even so, his Army lawyer was strong-willed and determined to win. Her name was Suzanne Schafer, and she was just as cold as the man himself. At one point, when all hope seemed to be lost on her end, she made a last-ditch effort to persuade the jury of her client's innocence. She took the stand, and what she said thereafter, I will never forget. "Look, she said, "here we have a minority company that was given a contract by the United States Army. It was a gracious contract, and it was gracious of the procurement department to award it to them. And now, it seems that they want us to pay them. Does that seem right to you?"

Joe Reeder interjected, "That's the most absurd thing I've ever heard in my life! It makes me ashamed to be associated with the military!"

The room went silent. After that, there were no more testimonies, and no more statements to be said. The jury retired and, only minutes later, came back with the verdict. They ruled in our favor.

It seemed that my dad's advice had paid off. Be persistent. Keep working hard. Although some people are mean-spirited, it doesn't mean you have to be too. I learned that day what he really meant when he said that. Sometimes you just need to ride it all out. Stick with your values and let things take their course. Sometimes you win, and sometimes you lose, but when you're persistent, you'll always come out better that you would have been by giving up.

Again, I was never bitter toward Mr. DeWitt. I could have chosen to be, with good reason, but I was raised to be better than that. In the end, it turned out that Mr. DeWitt was really just a nice man with corrupted values, and I know that because after the trial he immediately began changing his ways. Only six months later, when I returned to the base to check up on the network, I ran into him in the corridor.

"Joe Profit!" he said. "The minority businessman!"

"Hello, Mr. DeWitt," I kept my face low. He seemed to be acting a little too vibrant, so I was hesitant to go any further, but he just smiled at me and shook my hand.

"Joe," he said, "I really want to put everything we've been through behind us. That's where it belongs, anyway, right?" I nodded, and he continued, "So if you'd let me have the honor, I would love for you to join me at a barbecue I'm having tonight. All sorts of businessmen will be there, and I think you would fit right in."

"Are you serious?" By that time, I was just about ready for the prank to be revealed, but it never happened.

"I am serious," he said with the smile still pasted on his face, "I would love to be able to talk business with you, and I'm sure a lot of other people would as well."

I took Mr. DeWitt's offer, and less than a year after battling him to get on the military base, I attended a barbecue at his very own home, by his invitation. It was the most remarkable turnaround I had ever witnessed, and I believe it was by the strength of the Lord that he came to change. That is why I never count anyone out. I always believe that they have the ability to become good. In the meantime, I stay persistent, and wait until that day comes.

International Business Expansion

In the following years, Communications International kept growing at an overwhelming pace. INC Magazine named us one of the fastest growing privately held companies in America—for three years in a row! During that time, we grew over one thousand percent each year in our revenue, and I was named Minority Entrepreneur of the Year in a ceremony sponsored by Venture Magazine and Arthur Young & Company. I dedicated my award to the entire company for their tireless effort and genuine teamwork.

By the early 1990s we had established offices in over thirty cities in the United States, and ten countries in North America, Europe and the Middle East. Our main European office was located in downtown London, where we had hired a former president of Barclays Bank to run our finances.

Business could not have been better at that time. Communications International had quickly taken over my restaurants as the priority of my business, so I decided, with some hesitancy, to sell all of my restaurants back to their companies. From then on, I turned my focus explicitly to communications.

From London, we submitted a bid to supply our equipment and services to the government of Saudi Arabia. The job was to provide the Kuwait Oil Company (*a government-owned operation*) with an international telecommunications network. It was one of the largest jobs we had ever bid for, but we knew we had the resources, services and prices to make it happen.

Unfortunately, it didn't happen. Despite submitting the best bid, we were kicked out of the selection process early on without an explanation. In response, we submitted a second bid with an even better price.

Again, we were denied. It appeared that the government was opting for the work of larger companies, and did not take our bid seriously. The only company they were truly considering was AT&T.

By then, I had had enough of the nonsense. I protested against the operation and submitted an appeal to the government, stating that they were discriminating against the smaller companies. I showed our company's positive track record, and explained that we were clearly offering the best deal out of the competition. After the appeal, they re-opened the bidding process and CII submitted a third bid. At last, we were granted the job with no protest from the other companies.

The contract was a statement for both small business and minority businesses. It showed that we were able to compete with the larger companies, and provide quality business on an international scale. However, the main reason we ultimately got the job was not because we submitted the best offer. If it had been, we would have easily gotten the job after our first bid. Instead, we got the job because we showed persistence and determination. When we lost the first bid, we sent our best people to Riyadh, Saudi Arabia to set things straight. In doing so, we demonstrated that we cared deeply about every single job we bid for. The same could not be said for AT&T or any of the other large companies. It goes to show that determination and care are two of the best tools at your disposal, even when the competition appears to be bigger.

By the end of that year, CII had established itself as a prominent and powerful company in the Middle East, but business changed drastically when the Gulf War broke out. Suddenly, contracts were being handed out left and right to meet the demands of the United States government. Large American companies began migrating to Saudi Arabia and Kuwait. But the notable thing is that none of these companies were headed by minority CEOs. Before long, the issue gained worldwide media attention, and was displayed prominently on the Black Entertainment Television channel. Soon, the United States government was under fire from all corners of the nation.

At the time, I was serving as a member of the International Trade Board for Policy, and I got a call from Robert Mosbacher, the US Secretary of Commerce, who was looking for a solution to the problem.

I explained to the Secretary something that the minorities of the country already knew, "Mr. Mosbacher," I said, "The people are angry because we're fighting a war with black and brown people, but no black and brown people are making any money. It's all going to the white companies."

"So what can we do?" He said, "We're searching for minority American companies in the Middle East, but we can't find any over there."

"Well," I said, "We're over there." I explained the success that CII had had in the Middle East. I also explained that we were gaining traction in the telecommunications industry on a worldwide level, and we were gaining a good reputation along the way. "Is there any way we can help?" I asked.

"Well, the government is trying to clean up the oil fires in Kuwait right now. We can try to coordinate something with your company, if it's possible. I'll have to make some phone calls and see what I can do."

I was well aware of the oil fires. They were caused by the Iraqi military, and had been burning since January of that year, causing mass pollution and devastation throughout the small country of Kuwait. I didn't know how CII could be of any help, but I was willing to help if at all possible.

Later that same day, I received another call from Mr. Mosbacher. He told me that the military was in desperate need of telecommunications services in the oil fields. "The only available phone lines there are at risk of Iraqi eavesdropping, and all the other methods of communication are unreliable. Soldiers are in the middle of the desert, so there aren't a lot of options."

It didn't surprise me one bit. This was in the very early days of cell phones and the Internet, which made long distance communication a very difficult task. The fact that they were in the middle of the desert didn't seem to help. I told Mr. Mosbacher, "Our Company can fix that. You just give us the contract, and we'll provide you with everything you need."

"Joe," he said, "you need to know that this isn't a playground we're talking about. If you're going to set up a network for the military, it's going to need to be quick, efficient and effective, but most of all, it will need to be top secret. That means guaranteeing safety from eavesdropping."

"That's great," I said, "When can we start?"

Operation Phone Home

I already knew that Communications International had the materials to do exactly what Mr. Mosbacher was asking for, and I knew that we were exactly what he and his colleagues needed to escape from the criticism of the media. From that phone call forward, I knew the job was as good as ours.

In the following days, we finalized the contract with the United States government, Bechtel International and the Kuwait Oil Company to set up a mass communications network outside of Kuwait City—one that would give military personnel access to virtually any phone in the entire world, and provide voice, data and fax transmissions to personal computers around the globe. The contract was worth more than $50 million dollars—at the time, the largest contract ever given to a United States minority-owned company. As soon as the deal was finalized, we picked up our office in Saudi Arabia and moved it to Kuwait.

We sent our engineers into the oil fields to start setting up the network immediately. But we quickly learned that this was no ordinary operation. Working in the oil fields meant taking safety precautions like no other. Working with the military meant operating in complete stealth. It meant avoiding giving any indication to the Iraqis that we were setting up a network of any kind. To do this, we were forced to move outside of the oil fields to the barren wasteland of the Kuwait desert. From the middle of nowhere, we established telecenters, mobile telephones booth installed on flatbeds and inside tents that gave satellite access to the military phones. These were no ordinary telecenters. To avoid any possible chance of discovery, the telecenters had to be completely mobile. We had to build the receivers directly onto the military flatbed trucks. The result resembled some sort of alien spacecraft, with wires wrapped around the outside, and satellite dishes teeming from the beds in back. It was a makeshift operation, but it worked like a charm. From those mobile telecenters, we were able to provide communication on a global scale to the middle of the desert. With the technology available in the early 1990s, it was nothing short of a marvel. The operation was so successful, in fact, that upon completion we were immediately commissioned to expand the network to the military bases. They wanted everyone in the military, including the common soldier, to have the same phone access to anywhere in the world.

It captivated me on a personal level. I thought specifically of my dad, who, ages ago, was one of those "black and brown people" fighting hard for his country. In his day, it would have been impossible for him to call home from the war, but I know he would have given anything to do so. Well, now we had the technology. There was no hesitation for my next decision.

I met with the board of Youth United for Prosperity, a charitable program I had recently founded in Atlanta, devoted to helping the underprivileged youth in the community. I told them that I wanted to help the soldiers in Kuwait by providing them with free phone calls. There were no objections.

Once the network was up and running, we started donating

thousands of calling cards. Anytime a soldier wanted to make a call home to their family, they received one of our calling cards, absolutely free of charge. The program, dubbed as Operation Phone Home, provided the first free, uninterrupted link of communication between military personnel and their families—even when they were a world apart.

Back at home, the program received national acclaim. BET News broadcast our story to the entire country. In the segment, they praised our efforts as a step forward for black businessmen and women, and reminded the government that only good things could happen when they broadened their options to include minority-owned companies. It was a beautiful thing to hear. My goal was never to build confidence for the black community; it was simply to provide a service where it was needed. But once I realized the impact I had made, I felt blessed that I was able to help.

12 Twelve

LIFE KEEPS CHANGING

Growing Apart

In the business field, the work does not get easier as time goes by. There is never one "success", no matter how big, that alleviates you of your labor. No matter how successful you are, you have to keep working to make sure you don't stumble, because any stumble can lead to a downward spiral, and any past success can evaporate in the blink of an eye.

All of my companies were doing fine, and, financially, so was I. But I was struggling in another area of my life, one for which the same principle of continued hard work was even more applicable. It was about this time that my marriage with Deborah was hitting a speed bump. We had just brought our fourth child, Jessica into the world, but the two heads of the family were starting to break apart, which brought a crumbling effect to the entire unit.

I never, ever saw divorce as an option in my marriage. Growing up, I had always been taught that family was the most important thing in the world. When I gathered around the dinner table every evening, with my mom and dad both there, and my siblings surrounding me, I knew that I was among some of the only people that cared about me. I was among the people who believed in me and gave me the support that I needed. It played the single most important role in my success, and for that reason, I desperately wanted to provide the same experience for my children.

I tried hard to get my family back together. I felt that we had to work hard to work it out, but in the end I was the only one who felt that way, and Deborah and I were unable to reconcile. It seemed that I was pulling one way and she was pulling another. After more than twenty years together, we decided to get a divorce.

It was a sad time in my life—a time that weighed heavily on me emotionally. I was so distressed, because it was the very first time in my life that I knew I had failed. I had failed my wife, my kids, my parents and my God, and no matter how many successes I had in my life, the failure of my marriage did well to evaporate it all.

My pastor once told me that marriage is just like any team. Everyone involved needs to want to make it work and everyone involved needs to have the same goal. If one person gives up, or starts going for a different goal, the team falls apart and you're left with two individuals. In the end, that's how it was with Deborah and me. We were two individuals going for different goals.

In the wake of my divorce, I also realized how the hard work you put into something increases the amount of pain you feel when it fails. As a result, I decided that I would never put myself or anyone else through that kind of pain again. For the time being, I swore off marriage. I could not bring myself to pursue another relationship, because I feared that I would only hurt more people in the end.

I struggled for months trying to find a way to cope with the loss. This part was especially painful. In the past, whenever I needed encouragement, I would go to my family for support, but this time there was no one beside me to lend a helping hand. It felt like I was all alone, isolated in the corner of a dark room. I would go home at night and find an empty house, with nothing to offer me but the superficial comfort of material goods. Those things were able to satisfy me for a short amount of time, but in the end I realized that they were really just there to postpone the lonesome feeling that filled my heart.

I found what I lacked most was discipline. Without a strong woman by my side, I had no structure in my life. I had nobody to work for, nobody to provide for, and nobody to impress. The lack of discipline transcended into every facet of my life, so much so that I found it affecting my relationships and my business.

My son, Joseph Jr., who was visiting at the time, saw the pain that I was going through, so he tried to help me out. He suggested that I get into bodybuilding, something that he, as an athlete, was already doing. I took his advice and started going to the gym on a daily basis, with him by my side. Before long, I was reverting back to the ways of my football career. I discovered that bodybuilding—and more importantly, having a tangible goal that relied on continual improvement—helped to keep me strong physically and emotionally. It encouraged me to work hard in my business, my friendships and my relationships, and apply the same principle of continual improvement to those parts of my life.

Through our trips to the gym, Joseph and I were able to grow stronger in our relationship, too. We became each other's driving force—the encouragement we each needed to keep moving toward our goals. Before long, Joseph encouraged me to enter into competition. He convinced me that I was good enough to put my skills against the best in the business. I had never had the goal of competing, but as a gesture to him, I decided to give it a try. Well, it turned out that he was right. I began winning every meet in the Atlanta area. At the end of the year, I entered into The Masters Division—a national competition for men over forty—and I won!

Eventually, my son and I would travel around the globe for bodybuilding competitions on an international level. I never won any of those competitions, but the fact that I was there was an accomplishment to me. In fact, it was more than I had ever expected. I enjoyed every moment of it, most of all because I was able to prove to myself that I still had discipline, and that I still had the determination it took to succeed at something. I was able to prove to myself that I was still strong—physically and mentally—even in a time of emotional distress. That was the most important part. It was the only reason that I was able to keep my head up and eventually get back into the dating game.

I was divorced for ten years before I met my current wife, Wanda McVan. She and I met when I was in Monroe, Louisiana gathering information for a book we were making about my former coach, Mr. Patrick H. Robinson. Wanda was intrigued by the story, and we continued talking to each other after the event was over.

Later, I learned that she was working her way to Dallas, Texas in order to get a start on a modeling career. She also had an interest in business, which was intriguing to an entrepreneur like me.

But when she brought up dinner, and asked me if I would care to join her, I was taken back. Wanda projected such a youthful image, that I jokingly asked her for her identification- to find out her age.

Though she is almost twenty years my junior, she seemed much more mature than most women I knew.

We met at a local restaurant that night and had a great conversation. We talked about business, about life and about relationships. I explained my situation, and told her that I was not ready to begin dating again. All she said was, "I understand completely. I'm not ready to begin dating either." And ironically, we began dating not long after that.

I don't know how I was able to push through the events of my past. At the time, I really did feel like I wasn't prepared to care for another woman, and I didn't know if I ever would be. But the Lord energized me. As if my past failure was a film covering my eyes, He peeled it away and showed me that I was a strong, passionate and caring person. He showed me that I really was capable of loving a second time.

Though business kept us apart for days at a time, Wanda and I met up any time we could for nearly four years. We were very happy to have each other's company, but more importantly, we were happy to have each other's encouragement. We built each other up to be better people, and provided that same kind of structure that I had been missing in the aftermath of my divorce. But during that time together, we almost never mentioned the idea of marriage. It was something that was not even on our radar screen. We were still two individuals working toward individual goals, and we were happy with that. It wasn't until the end of the four years that we realized neither of us was going to leave the other anytime soon. Again, it was as though we each gave a shrug of the shoulder and said, "Well, why not?" After four years of dating, we finally decided to take the plunge and marry.

It may have taken a long time for it to happen, but I know those four years leading up to our marriage were meaningful. In that time, we truly got to know each other—something that is necessary for such a large commitment.

Marriage, to me, is the mortar of our society. It holds us all together. I believe there is nothing more special than a union between two people who strive to make each other better. But along with the happiness that it can bring, marriage is also something you have to work at. It's hard, and you need to put all of your effort, determination and motivation into it, otherwise it will crumble and fall.

As stated before, when my first marriage came to a close, it was the only time in my life when I felt like I had truly failed. For years, that did a number on me. But God was gracious in giving me a second chance to mend the mistakes and pitfalls from that marriage. He showed me the right way to make a marriage succeed, and for that, I am forever grateful. In the same manner that I had done all my life, I was once again able to turn my roadblocks into stepping stones.

I learned from my mistakes and I moved forward. Now, as I enter the sixteenth year of my marriage with Wanda, I can proclaim loudly, and honestly, that I am a very happy family man.

13 Thirteen

Searching for True Success

Giving Back

Family, to me, is a way of sharing the joy in your life with other people. The ultimate goal is to love one another and care for one another. I believe the same can be said not only about families, but about communities. This is why charity work has played such an important role in my life. It is my biggest passion, and it is what I devote my life to today.

The first time I got involved in charity work was back in 1972 when I was coming off of my knee injury with the Falcons. I had learned of a recreation center called Pittman Park, which was located in a disadvantaged area of Atlanta. Their goal was to provide the youngsters of the neighborhood with a safe haven—a place where they could go to participate in activities and learn lessons that promote a positive lifestyle. I signed up to help out in my spare time, and used my upbringing to my advantage. Through the stories I told of my own life—many of which you've read in this book—I was able to relate to the kids.

I found that a lot of what they needed was not money, but rather a person to care about them. After I started working with the kids, I realized how important figures like us are in their lives. You don't have to be an athlete or a movie star to make a difference. You just need to give your time.

When I look back at the atmosphere in which I grew up, I see a community that did not have a lot of money, I see families that did not have a lot of material possessions, and I see schools that could not afford the right materials for their classrooms. But somehow, despite all that, we were able to succeed. Why were we able to succeed?

I believe it was because of our spirit. The fact of the matter is that our lack of possessions only brought us closer together. In those times of struggle, we learned to rely on one another, to provide for one another, and to be a family.

The Business Management Program and Youth United for Prosperity

And so, because of this, I decided that I wanted to devote myself to helping others create that same special atmosphere. In 1975, I teamed up with the NFL for their new Business Management Program. The program was headed by Buddy Young—the assistant commissioner of the NFL at the time under Pete Rozelle—with the goal of getting underprivileged high school students involved in the business world. The problem was that there were many athletes from low-income towns that also suffered from low expectations. Because of this, many of them would never even think twice about getting a chance in the business world. Having witnessed the benefits of high expectations first-hand in my home town, I felt that I could help push the students in the right direction. Mr. Young hired fifteen NFL players to head the program. These players were also from lower-income towns, and among them was James 'Shack' Harris—another Monroe, Louisiana native who had grown up right alongside me.

As a team, we travelled around the country and met with CEOs from dozens of corporations. Our job was to convince them to hire lower-income student-athletes from their area in hopes of them gaining positive, healthy experience in a business setting. The catch was that these students had to be in the top 10% of their high school class, and they had to be in good behavioral standing. Our hope was that we could inspire young students to work hard so they could be in that top 10% and be able to get a glimpse of the payoff that awaited in the business world.

The program became very successful once the CEOs realized that they could benefit from it too, by raising the students in their environment for full-time hire later on. Because of this, we started a partnership with the National Alliance of Businessmen, who helped bring hundreds of otherwise underprivileged students into a prosperous environment. Shack and I ran offices in both Atlanta and New Orleans, and together we succeeded in bringing more students to the business world than all of the other members of the program combined.

The program had an impact that would last longer than its own tenure. Not only were there many students directly affected by its benefits, but I was affected as well. Later on, I would use the skills and knowledge that I learned from the Business Management Program for good use in starting my own national 501(c) (3) charity organization, Youth United for Prosperity, Inc. (YUP).

I founded YUP with one purpose in mind, and that purpose can be found in the name. I wanted to bring the youth together to promote a healthy community—one that would build, grow and prosper. The foundation had principles that drew from my time with Pittman Park, The Business Management Program and my own experiences.

The YUP programs still exists today. Ever since the foundation began in the early '90s, we have grown and spread across the entire nation, using our stories and lessons to motivate youth to dream big. It's a message that those young individuals need to hear.

YUP has also created a number of registered trademarks through many of its programs within its own structure, including LEGENDS & KIDS®, PROPLAYERS & ENTERTAINERS NETWORK® —which devotes it's time to helping kids pursue successful careers—and the PRIDE Institute—which pairs youngsters with a professional or college athlete as a mentor, in hopes that both will grow through the program's motto: Professional Results In Daily Efforts™.

One of the most stimulating programs that YUP have created today is the LEGENDS & KIDS® Young Authors Program. The program and its vision has resulted from my personal experience, with a large number of kids that needed some type of excitement and motivation from something other than sports and games. This project gives children who may not excel in athletics an opportunity to excel in academic and other area such as illustrating, graphic design, computer technology and creativity.

The projects builds pride, confidence, and self-esteem as the students realize that they can excel in areas other than sports and be just as important as their friends who excelled in sports. This project has been proven and increased writing scores on assessment test and has turn students that are future dropouts into successful students with future goals and achievements.

The YUP program that means the most to me on a personal level is the Adopt-a-Town Program. Through this program, we were able to sponsor the entire town of Lake Providence, Louisiana—my original hometown. Originally, we travelled to Lake Providence with a mission to help just one school, but when we returned to the town, we saw that the whole community was in desperate need of attention. With the help of the Atlanta Chapter of the NFL Alumni, we returned to Lake Providence to announce that we had "adopted" the entire town. Ever since, YUP has been building its relationship with Lake Providence, slowly transforming my former home into a brighter community.

Today, I still dedicate a large portion of my time ensuring that these and other charities succeed. I serve as president of YUP as well as the NFL Alumni Atlanta Chapter, both of which frequently join hands in running successful charity events round the country.

But these blessings did not come through works of mine alone. They came through many people who have supported me and my efforts. My mother and father are my biggest influences. They're the strongest people I've ever known. When I was a young boy, I saw them break their backs so that my siblings and I could have the life we have today. Together, they kept going through the pain. They kept fighting, they kept believing, and they never lost faith that today would be better than tomorrow.

By God's blessing, I have been able to help many underprivileged people who have shared the trials and roadblocks that I have. But while I was blessed to have two people in my family that supported me—and many more in the community—there are countless youngsters that I've encountered over the years don't have a single person. Without our help, they will fail to see what God's plan for them really is. I urge those of you reading to heed the call to make a difference in the lives of others. You may think you don't have the time or the resources, but you do. As my pastor once said, "You always have the time, but you choose to spend it on something else. You always have the resources, but you choose to use them for other things." So don't let your own life trickle by without giving an effort to better the lives of others. There are always people close by that needs the support that you can provide. Just think, maybe you can be the driving force for the success in someone else's life.

Choosing Success / Chosen for Success

I feel like success can be defined in a lot of ways. It is, perhaps, one of the most subjective concepts in the entire world, because we all see it through different lenses that have forged by every facet of our lives. Many people see the word success and immediately think of money. "He runs a million-dollar company," they say, "He must be a successful man." Others view success as a gain of power, noting, "Whoever controls the world will be successful in getting what they want." Some people view success as a comparison to others. If they are better than the majority, they are successful in that field. Some people view success as an intangible quality, such as happiness, comfort, security or tranquility.

I believe it's a good thing that we have so many definitions of success. In fact, we can learn a lot about the world and about each other if we listen to each other's unique definitions. But I think there is one overarching quality that can be found—however slightly—in every single definition in the world. It is the quality of overcoming a challenge through adversity.

I've brought it up many times already, and I'll bring it up once more. My high school football coach, Mackie Freeze, said, "When you run into a road block, you stare it straight in the face. You tell it that you're not going to be swayed, 'cause you're stronger than that roadblock. You make sure it's watching as you place your foot on its face and turn it into a stepping stone." To me, that is the ultimate realization of success.

So then, the question for me is, "Can I consider myself successful?"

As I ponder this question, I like to look back to the time and place from which I started. As a boy, I grew up and lived with ten other people under the same dilapidated roof. The house itself was in a neighborhood that wasn't any better. To pay for our food, we worked in the fields that sliced our hands and burned our backs, and we'd come home at night with nothing to look forward to but the hope of a better tomorrow. How I remember the face of my mother as she cooked our meals. Her eyes were sunken and exhausted, wondering when she would have enough food to feed her hungry children. We never had money for anything other than food.

But with all the hardships and poverty that encased my life back then, there came good things that made us wealthy. For one, we were wealthy in pride. I saw it in my father's work. After so many days and years in the field, he still bundled up his crops with the same energy that he did when he first started. He knew he didn't have the best work in the world, but he knew when he'd done a good job. I always admired him for that.

We were rich in confidence. The only way that that could have happened was if it started from the ground up. It started again with my parents, who had so much confidence in each one of us that they were willing to send us to college—an immense financial toll—rather than keep us at home to earn money. Out of all nine children, five graduated from college and all of us received a job with financial security.

We were rich in hope. Growing up in Monroe, it was easy for us to see the distinction between the rich and the poor. It was easy to look up at the big buildings and let them tower over us, intimidate us and make us feel insignificant. But I was never taught to view it that way. I was taught to look up at the big buildings in awe, and dream of one day being there beside them. I was taught to dream of being in a better place, of breaking free from my neighborhood's shackles and rise up above the low expectations of the world.

I look back at those times, then, and ask myself, "What has come of it all?" I look to every field of life for answers.

First, I look to the field of business, and consider all that I have accomplished there. I have run a wide scope of financially successful restaurants. I have built a company, Communications International, Inc. that rose through the ranks to become one of the most profitable telecommunications firms in the world. In turn, that company has helped the country's government and military benefit from greater security, access and affordability. It has helped make communication easier than ever before for the men and women who were at service overseas. Today, CII lives strong as a merged entity of the Multimedia

Digital Broadcasting Corporation—an internet communications firm for which I serve as founder, President and CEO. In addition to my own businesses, I have served as the chairman of Blacks for Reagan/Bush. I have served as a member of the International Trade Commission (appointed by President Reagan and later President Bush, Sr.), as well as the Small Business Advisory Board, the Department of Transportation Advisory Board, and the Federal Communications Commission. In 1994, as a result of my tireless efforts, I was inducted as a lifetime member into the Business and Professional Hall of Fame (also known as America's Best and Brightest Businessmen).

I look to what I have accomplished outside of the business field. Because of my financial earnings, I have been able to give back to the community on a grand scale. Through the Youth United for Prosperity (YUP) programs, my colleagues and I have helped thousands of kids gain a positive influence from the members of their community, and get a head start on finding true success in their own lives. We have traveled to several historically-impoverished towns and cities throughout the South. Some of the places we visited included my birth place of Lake Providence, Louisiana, Anniston, Bessemer and Dadeville Alabama. We provided those communities with an outlet of faith, hope and inspiration-the same qualities of the community that I admired and embraced as a child.

I look to my family-the most important thing in the world. First, I ask myself, "Have I made my mom and dad proud?" They never stopped working for a better life for me and my siblings. Though it has been a struggle (and it always will be, no matter what), I have used the lessons they taught me as tools in my journey, and I have built myself a better, happier and more prosperous life. Now that I have children of my own- all of whom have grown into wonderful adults- and as I continue to raise and inspire them, the virtues of my parents will continue to flow through me and be passed down to them. I know that I have made my parents proud. I look to my community. Wow. Words cannot do justice to the change racial inequality that this country-this national community-has undergone since I was young boy with blistered hands full of cotton. And my mom knew it all along that it would happen. She always reassured me, as she held me tight in her arms, "You better believe thing's will get better, Joe. Just be strong in your work, strong in your spirit, and strong in your faith. Things will get better."

From my childhood, to my adolescence, to my early adulthood, to this very day, I have kept her words by my heart. I have challenged the world, and I have stood tall in the face of adversity, even when I was the only one standing. I have turned my roadblocks into stepping stones and persevered, from the streets, to the countryside, to the courthouse, to the jail cell, and to the university that seemed like hell.

When I started my journey at Northeast, I was the scapegoat of the white world. Fifteen years after graduation, I returned to campus to deliver the commencement speech to the graduating class. At the end of my speech, I received a standing ovation—the first in the history of the university. On that day, I saw another glimpse of what my mom was talking about. Through the power of the Lord, we have come far as a nation, and we will forever continue to get better.

When I look back at all of these accomplishments, and then look at my own definition of success—overcoming challenges through adversity—I must say that I have met the challenge and overcome adversity in all fields of life. Through the help of countless other people, through the help of the Lord in Heaven, and through struggle, strife and perseverance, I consider myself successful in all fields of life.

So now the question turns to you. Can you consider yourself successful?

For so much of this book, I've written about having high expectations, both from others and from yourself, so that you may accomplish great things. But what if meeting those expectations is only the bare minimum? What if you made the decision to exceed those expectations? If it weren't possible, there would be a lot of hopelessness in the world, and my story would have no effect on my readers. In reality, expectations are just that—expectations—and nothing more. They're fabrications of the mind, and they don't exist in the real world. When you're setting expectations for yourself, all you're doing is putting a limit on you and your abilities. In reality, the only way to know your limits is to test them.

It is my hope that this book has painted a picture of someone who has met the expectations of the world and exceeded them. It is also my hope that I have inspired you to live out that example in your own life, by turning your roadblocks into stepping stones and exceeding all the expectations around you. There are successes out there waiting to be performed! There are miracles out there waiting to happen! So go set the bar infinitely high, and then reach higher than that! Go make a positive difference in the world. Live as an example for others so you can inspire them to do the same. And most importantly, never, ever stop growing!

This has been a long, sometimes tiring and sometimes hard, journey for me, but it is a journey that was filled with hope, thanks to my parents and other influential people in my life. It continues to be so. And just as I made it, you can too. May God bless all of you!

14 Fourteen

PROFIT'S VIEWS ON LIFE IN THE BUSINESS WORLD

"Professional Sports is a Business...Not A Lifestyle"

Creating A Life Game Plan

This section of the book is meant to be a guide for those of you trying to pursue athletics as a profession. While that is the main focus, the guide itself is not only for athletes. It can be for anyone who is looking to get into the business field. This guide is meant to encourage you to start acting before you get out of your current field (whether it is school, athletics or a job), and to organize a plan that will keep you financially healthy. These are my rules for life in the business world.

Develop an ongoing "Life Game Plan"

There's an adage that says "Nobody plans to fail, they simply fail to plan." In the following chapter, I'll touch on what it means to have a Life Plan. The basic principle, though, is to have a map of how you envision your life for the many years to come. You'll find that your life is a whole lot easier when you know your destination ahead of time.

As you construct your Life Plan, you'll want to make sure that you put it down on paper. If you keep it in your head, it's only fiction, but if you write it down then it becomes tangible.

A true Life Plan not only lays out your goals, it lays out the things you need to start doing now, while you're still in the game.

Get a College Degree

Some people in today's world underestimate the power of a college degree. They're cynical about its powers to actually help you make money. But in reality, these are the people that have fallen victim to poor financial planning. They go into school thinking the bills will magically pay themselves off someday, without ever planning a savings account ahead of time. It's true that college is expensive, but the bills can be managed with proper planning. Make sure going into school that you'll be able to pay off your debts. Avoid excessive spending, too. I've seen so many people think that a school loan is a license to spend. Remember my story at Alcorn State? I couldn't even get a box fan in my room. Today, there are countless students on government assistance that own big screen TVs and expensive cars. Not only is this an unethical way to spend, but it will ruin you at the end of your college career.

Getting through school and earning a degree is the only thing that will get you a white collar job. Even if you've built a strong foundation of skills in athletics, nobody will give you a second look if they don't know that you can perform elsewhere. Today, even a bachelor's degree is no guarantee you'll find a good job. A master's degree is the bare minimum for a high-paying job in the business world. Even if you're planning on pursuing sports as a profession, make a plan to finish your schooling—if not now, then immediately after your athletic career. Smart athletes do this all the time. After retiring from the NFL, Troy Aikman went back to UCLA to finish his final year of college. While he was still playing in the NBA, Shaquille O'Neal went to college online. He studied and took classes while he traveled the country with his team, and recently earned his Ph.D. superstars like Troy and Shaq will always have opportunities open for them, but now their opportunities cover a much wider spectrum.

College degrees are more than just an acquisition of knowledge. They are a demonstration to your employer or investors that you are committed to success, that you have a strong work ethic, and that you've both set goals and achieved them. A degree tells them that you are serious about competing and growing.

Develop A Personal Brand

Are you writing this down? I hope you are, because this rule is one of the most important. Prepare your brand. What do I mean by brand? Well, your brand is your image. It's how you present yourself to the world. It shows your character, your work ethic, your habits—both good and bad—and your personality. Your brand starts being molded from the day you learn to talk, so you need to take special care of it.

If you don't take precious care of your brand, it will lead you into social and financial destruction. You'll find it harder to get a job. You'll find it harder to land endorsement deals. There are two great examples that come to mind. The first is Michael Vick. Before being arrested for his acts of animal cruelty, he was one of the highest paid athletes on the planet. But most of his money came from outside of his salary. As soon as he hit the jail cell, he was dropped from sponsors like Nike and Powerade. While in jail, his more than $100 million dwindled down to nothing, and he had to file for bankruptcy.

The second example is Michael Phelps. As an Olympic athlete, he made nearly all of his money from endorsement deals, but many of his sponsors dropped him immediately after he was caught on camera using drugs. Not only did he lose endorsements, but he was suspended from professional swimming. Phelps had a lapse in judgment, and a simple photo was enough to lose him a whole lot of money.

The idea itself is simple. Do anything you can to protect your brand. Develop a persona that does not define you by your job, but your personality. Your brand will stay with you forever, and you'll find that the seemingly insignificant things (or, the things you think nobody will ever find out about) can come back to bite you. So prepare your brand immediately, before you leave your field. Don't let anyone tarnish the reputation that you're trying to mold.

Stay Out of Trouble with the Law

At any level of business, fame, or popularity, a bad image is a repellent for business; nevertheless, there will be others trying to tarnish your image. They do this for selfish reasons, usually because they have something to gain. Whether you're doing anything wrong or not, the image that someone else projects to others will be the ultimate factor in your image. It's like a rumor spreading through high school. Once it picks up momentum, it's nearly impossible to refute.

The best way to combat this is to stay out of anything that can be perceived as bad, even if you don't think it's harmful. Don't associate with other people or places that can ruin your image. Employers are looking for people with a spotless reputation. When working with young people, I always tell them, "Live like you're running for president. The slightest bump can send your campaign out of control." Do not expect to get the job or get the deal if you even associate with trouble.

Develop a Life Time Network While You're in the Game

If you ask any former football player what he misses most about the game, he'll tell you that it's the locker room, the camaraderie and the bonding. When you're in a field like athletics, the time of bonding is a God-given time for networking. This is a time when you can build relationships with all sorts of people—teammates, coaches, executives, anyone—that have the potential to last a lifetime. The beautiful thing is that these people will all eventually move on to other walks of life. They will spread out across the world and across all different types of fields. You need to use this time of networking to your full potential—building relationships that you'll keep rather than let fade away.

Back when I was a Falcon, and I waited outside Rankin Smith's office every day. It was hard at first to make a connection, especially with the inherent division between employer and employee, but I was determined. We eventually established a relationship, and Mr. Smith was able to help give me a foothold that would launch me into my future business endeavors. I owe a large amount of my financial success to the network I established with Mr. Smith and his colleagues.

I see each person I meet as a door. When I sever a connection, it closes that door and I've lost all benefits that come with knowing that person. Networking is an incredibly important principle and skill to learn—and yes, networking does take skill. Some have it naturally, but for others it is harder to recognize the benefits of connections. For those of you who may have trouble, there is a simple philosophy that will help get you started: Never, ever close a door if you don't have to.

Tips for networking:

- Always be polite and courteous
- Never refuse to sign autographs
- Make connections with the team owners and upper management. They usually have very large networks already, and they can help pull some weight with others.
- Get to know the former player on your team
- Join the Chamber of Commerce
- Donate time to Charitable organizations
- Keep as many doors open as possible.
- Establish connections with people outside of your social network. You never know who they might have in their network.
- If you meet someone new, try to obtain and retain their contact information. If you get to know them better, ask about their family, friends and employment. Take note of these. Each new person is a new open door.
- Don't just keep the doors open, but open new ones as well. Instead of telling someone, "Thank you for talking," say "Thank you for talking. Is there any way I can stay in touch?"
- If you're denied a position of employment, don't close the door. Keep it open at least a crack, and say, "May I try to reach you again at a later date?" Persistence goes a long way in showing someone that you mean business.

Risk-Taking

A trend among athletes is to branch out into other business endeavors such as restaurants, car dealerships and franchises. Many of them are successful, especially when the athlete brandishes the company with his or her own name. Businesses such as these can be a healthy form of finance and recreation, but they also raise a risk that is meant to be taken very seriously.

As much as there is to gain from these businesses, athletes have lost a lot due to poor planning. Deuce McAllister, the Saints all-time leading rusher, for instance, owed $6.5 million to Nissan for a failed car dealership.

It can be dangerous to assume just because you have a big name in one field that you can succeed in any field you'd like. But this is not the case. As much as we would like to believe it, athletes are not impervious to financial failure. My advice is to hire a trusted management team that will be able to watch over your business while you are dealing with your primary career. In searching for your team, you should check out their track record, look at their past performance with other clients.

Prepare for the Transition Ahead of Time

There is no question that this is a difficult transition. The problem is that many of us fool ourselves into thinking there will be some high-paying job waiting for us at the other end. We graduate from school, receive the diploma, then walk off the stage and realize there's nothing on the other side. The cold of the world starts to seep in, and we look desperately for shelter.

For me, the transition came much earlier than I was hoping for. I could have drowned myself in pity, but thankfully I had planned ahead. I had done all of the things that I just laid out. I had gotten my college degree before playing in the NFL. I had kept my brand clean; I had stayed out of trouble, and I had established a network with the players and executives.

Even with all these preparations, the transition out of the game—at such an early age—took a financial and emotional toll. But because I had planned ahead, I was blessed enough to be able to support my starting family while looking toward life after the game.

The main thing to remember is that athleticism is not much of a transferable skill. Unless you stay in the field, you won't be using it a lot. Here we're talking about transitioning away from the field anyway, so it becomes obsolete altogether.

Find your strengths ahead of time. If you pay attention, your skills will reveal themselves to you in your daily life. But it's your job to employ them.

At a young age, I realized my skills for business. I was good at networking, and when I realized that I wanted to be a businessman, I started using my networking skills to make sure I found anyone I could that knew anything about the field of business. Even while I was still in high school, my football coach—the only CPA in town—saw my passion for business and what it could potentially evolve into. He started making more connections for me, and helped set the course for my life as a businessman.

Know Your Value

At the end of the day, you know what you're worth. Nobody else defines you. Your parents, your friends, your town—they influence you but they do not determine who you are. Since growing up in the poorest parish in the entire country, I have learned a thing or two about finding my own value. It all comes from within, so if you know what you're capable of, don't let anyone or anything get in the way. Confront your obstacles head on.

15 Fifteen

Profit's View on Economics

How to Avoid Financial Ruin as a Professional Athlete

So far, I have told you my life story. I have shown you that there is hope for anyone determined enough to achieve success in all the fields of life. If you are ready to take that challenge and stare your obstacles in the eye, then this chapter is for you. In this chapter, I have laid out my rules for achieving financial success in the world of professional sports—a world that is full of potential earnings, but saturated with potential destruction.

Establish a Good Credit Score

Do not burden yourself with any unnecessary debt unless you have a reasonable expectation of a sustainable income stream either from your investments, business, or your other reliable source. Sometimes debt is necessary in order to establish a good credit.

Banks routinely approve pro athletes and entertainers for mortgages. Even with today's tightened regulations, they are eager to lend money for cars, boats, jewelry, businesses and investment real estate. If you earn enough to quality for the financing, accept it with much caution, do not over extend yourself. A great deal of pro athletes and entertainers end up in bankruptcy court. Here are a few word of caution: Take heed -never file for bankruptcy if you do not have any money coming in or money to live on.

Develop Good Saving Habits and Have an Adequate Cash Reserve

Most pro athletes will not find the kind of salary that they are accustomed to in the open market. They cannot predict the amount of time it will take from the time they leave the NFL until the time they have secured a steady income stream that will sustain their lifestyles. Players typically burn through their severance in the first year and then start depleting their savings and investments while they try to establish themselves in the business world. You must plan for the worst case scenario and aim to pleasantly surprise yourself.

Avoid Taking too Many Risks

As I said earlier, it is important to know the deals you're getting into. Only by gaining knowledge of our business deals can we significantly reduce the risk factor. One of my best friends once lost a lot of money when he purchased a local restaurant in his home town. The previous owners had been in the business for many years, but after only a year under my friend's ownership it went out of business. The problem was that he had no experience or training, and he did not invest any time in the business. As a result, he lost everything.

As professional athletes, we tend to be very confident individuals, and often too confident. Night clubs, restaurants, real estate ventures, and franchise opportunities are all extremely risky business propositions. Worse yet, they require substantial expertise in legal, accounting, tax, management, operations, marketing, human resources, and sales. When you invest in a business, never forget that you are choosing to compete against the sharpest entrepreneurs on the planet. Very few of us possess the skills required to compete successfully in the business world while we are in the professional sports, or shortly thereafter. If you want to invest in a business, be certain you have acquired the prerequisite skills. Do not just jump into it.

Obtain Business Network Development

Just because you know someone well enough to trust them does not mean they have the expertise required to advise you or manage your affairs. Far too many NFL players have been burned by very well-meaning, good-hearted, and trustworthy people who simply were not qualified to give proper advice. Surround yourself with qualified and experienced advisors in taxes, finance, business, legal matters, real estate, or whatever you are involved in. Never hire anyone who is not legally obligated to uphold the fiduciary standard.

Become Involved in Your Finances

Do not fall into the trap of thinking that the money will magically manage itself. This is not true. Even the highest earners have hit rock bottom because they haven't had the right people helping them make decisions.

Setting up a team of advisors is the first step you should take once you're anticipating a big paycheck. You will need to acquire one or more advisors who have experience in large sums of money (not only should they have experience, but also success). These people will be there to make sure you know what you're doing with your money. Your advisors need to be ethical and competent people who will prepare an ongoing strategy of wealth management that will provide a quality lifestyle long after the game.

Once you have a team of financially sound advisors, you'll need to start learning how to use your money. Now, you may not like that idea right away. Most people want to make a big purchase once they break the bank for the first time. Don't worry—we'll get to the "fun money" later on—but you have to remember that you won't always be breaking the bank, so you need to set up an ongoing plan for success that involves good investments.

Athletes should understand how their money is being managed and invested. You now have a team of advisors, so ask them questions. How is my money being invested? Why are these investments good for me? Are you investing any of your money in the same projects? Insist that your advisors provide you with a financial statement and have them explain the statement. You'll need to know what is going on with your money on a quarterly basis (at least four times per year).

Avoid "Sure Things"

If you earn a large salary, chances are that other people will know that you earn a large salary. This means that you will quickly become the target of unscrupulous pitches for an investment. They'll tell you that you are guaranteed a certain sum of money in return, but they will quickly run away and you will likely never see a cent again.

No matter what's the size of your salary; the key is to avoid sure things. In that regards, my motto is, "If it sounds too good to be true, it probably is." Many people will try to convince you that you don't have enough money. They'll use tactics to trick you into thinking that you are not adequate. Try to stray away from this type of thinking.

Keep in mind that your money is safe as long as it's in your control.

Develop Good Saving and Spending Habits

Do not spend like there's no tomorrow. The greatest folly in money management is spending money before having a plan in place. Buying a house, a car or other luxuries—these are things we want to do right away to soak up the good life, but without a plan, your spending can get out of hand far too quickly.

I remember when I first started making good money in football, I wanted to turn around and give back to my family, who had helped me so much growing up. A lot of athletes have this tendency, because a lot of athletes come from the same kind of places that I did, and have never seen that kind of wealth before. But there are certain variables that need to be taken into account before you start spending.

The first is taxes. Roughly 50 percent of your first paycheck will go to the government. In other words, if your salary if $5 million, you're really making $2.5 million. Keep in mind that there are certain ways to lessen your tax burden, while making money from investments in the meantime.

After taxes come other liabilities. Are you still in debt from previous schooling, mortgages, rent or credit cards? These things must be taken care of immediately. You cannot push them off until later, believing there will be some magical time when the stars align and you truly have enough to pay those things off. Instead, you need to set up a plan where you can reasonably pay off your debts over time. Get them done with and out of the way as early as possible. It will free up your money for spending later on. Debt can be a good thing in order to build up a healthy credit score, but you should not go into debt if you cannot back it up.

Lastly, you need, need, need to set aside money for savings. Not only should you start saving for retirement, but also for the unexpected events that could throw you off your rail. You never know what will lie ahead in your career. If a linebacker falls down on your knee and kills your career, will you have anything left to tide you over? Planning for the unexpected is not only smart, but it relieves a lot of stress that comes from the uncertainties in life.

After taxes and debts are taken care of, a certain amount of your paycheck can be set aside for "fun money". It may not be as much as you wanted, but it's certainly the smartest and most stable way to go while planning for the future. This is your allowance, just like when you were a child. Once that money's gone, there's no more touching it.

So many people trust their salary as their omnipotent higher being, but the salary has a tendency to disappear. Just keep in mind that if you spend wisely, you'll be able to spend more and spend better.

Be Aware of the Benefits Available to You

With any sport—whether it be football, baseball, basketball, hockey, soccer, golf or whatever—there will be more opportunities available to you. You're one in a million, now. You're making the big money, and now you've got benefits you never dreamed of. Some people say once you become a superstar, you'll never have to buy a drink again. But there are more benefits for you than the bar room perks.

Remember earlier when I told you to set aside 50 percent of your salary for taxes? You probably groaned, and maybe even smacked the book closed right there. Well, the good news is that sports salaries are W-2s, which means there are ways to get tax breaks and avoid paying such absurd totals year after year.

Investing is the way to do this. In fact, the government likes it when you invest, because it puts money directly into their economy. Why would you want to pay taxes when you can put it toward creating jobs, helping people and bettering the community? Regardless of the size of your paycheck, you'll find that giving money and avoiding taxes is a way that everyone comes out better.

But when you hear the word "investment", you probably picture a Wall Street, risk-reward-type atmosphere. This doesn't have to be the case. You can invest your money practically anywhere and it can help you avoid taxes. You can give to companies, charities, religious organizations, or anything that is tax deductible. If you have questions, ask a financial advisor, and learn the ways you can reduce your taxes and put your money to good use.

Engage in Family Management Planning

This is an area that people like to avoid. It's awkward to sit down and arrange a contract with your family. Naturally, you won't want to write up a "divorce clause" at a time when you're preparing to embark on a happy, healthy marriage.

Unfortunately, unanticipated breaks in families happen, and many wealthy people have endured significant losses due to familial disputes. In situations like these, it's important to remember one very tried and true fact: It's not about how much you make, it's about how much you keep.

Divorce rates are disproportionately high in the years following retirement, and the loss of wealth that comes along with divorce (including child care and loss of joint assets) is tolling on both parties. You may not want to believe it, but direct and firm family planning is a necessary step to avoid financial ruin.

For your best interest, you need to manage everything. Insist on a prenuptial agreement, including clauses for children and assets. Get a lawyer to look over your agreement and see that it is structurally sound. Negotiate the situation with your spouse—with any luck, they'll be happy to have an agreement in place as well. Do anything you can to make sure you have a plan in place ahead of time.

Nurture Family Relationships

There is no question that transitioning out of the Professional sports is a difficult process. However, do not forget that it is equally (if not more) difficult for our spouses and significant others. Just like us, our spouses lose their social network, their sense of belonging, and part of their identity. And after watching us thrive as strong, confident warriors in sports, they may see our vulnerable side as we transition to our new lives. Rather than confront these challenges together, couples often turn away from each other and toward others during the transition. Unfortunately, that is often the beginning of the end of their relationship. Divorce is devastating both financially and emotionally. Be brave enough to open up to your spouse and seek his or her help as you navigate your transition. Conquering this challenge together may very well bring you closer than ever.

Develop another outlet for competitive drive

Nobody survives in the NFL without having an ultra-competitive drive. Unfortunately, unlike other sports, once we retire from football, it is simply impossible to continue to play recreationally. The challenge is to find another outlet for your athletic competitive drive. Find another sport to compete in…perhaps something completely different from your original sport. Some find great satisfaction in coaching. Commit yourself to getting good at it. Seek mentorship from someone who has mastered the sport then train just as hard as you did for your original sport. You will be amazed at how fulfilling it is to begin to master a brand new task. (In my case it was body building, and I took it seriously and it took me all the way to national and international competition).

Define Yourself a After the Game

This is the last rule I have, but it is one of the most important. The definition of self determines who we become after we've transitioned out of the game. For most of our lives, the world has defined us as athletes. Many of us buy into this idea, and cling to our former selves entirely too long after our playing days are over. Yes, we should all be proud of our careers, but when it's all said and done, we need to begin the process of re-defining who we really are, perhaps for the first time in our lives.

This process begins with a tremendous about of soul searching to decide who it is you really want to be. Eventually, you will need to psychologically shed the moniker of "professional athlete" and start to take on new labels—labels that have to do with who you are as a person, such as great parent, inspiring coach or excellent friend.

I would like to quote a line from Hall of Famer, Jim Brown in 'Any Given Sunday'… "When a man looks back on his life, he should be proud of all of it…not just the time he spent in pads and cleats."

Made in the USA
Charleston, SC
18 January 2013